The Woman Who Wouldn't Stop Writing

The Woman Who Wouldn't Stop Writing

Hannah More

Sarah Allen

CF4•K

For my dear daughters,
Maisy and Jemimah

10 9 8 7 6 5 4 3 2 1

Copyright © 2014 Sarah Allen

Paperback ISBN 978-1-78191-523-3

epub ISBN 978-1-78191-533-2

mobi ISBN 978-1-78191-536-3

Published by Christian Focus Publications,
Geanies House, Fearn, Tain, Ross-shire,
IV20 1TW, Scotland, U.K.
Tel: +44 (0)1862 871011
Fax: +44 (0)1862 871699
www.christianfocus.com
email: info@christianfocus.com

Cover design by Daniel van Straaten
Cover illustration by Jeff Anderson
Printed and bound in Denmark by Nørhaven

Contents

Why Hannah More?...................................... 6

The First School 7

New Plans 15

Drama! 21

Love Story 29

Escape to London..................................... 39

A New Book... 49

Trying Hard 59

Changing the World 67

Back to School 77

Runaways and Revolutions 85

More Stories.. 95

The Final Chapter 105

Postscript 113

Thinking Further Topics 114

About the Author 122

Did You Know?... 123

Hannah Moore Timeline............................... 126

Why Hannah More?

When I was a little girl I wanted to be a writer. I would write poems and stories in notebooks and hide them away. Now that I'm grown-up I have five children who all love reading and writing too. So when I first found out about Hannah More, who had once been a little girl writing stories in secret, I was hooked. Finding out about her wasn't easy though, in fact it has been quite a challenge. Not many people know about her, and you can't buy books about her or by her in the shops. Detective work was required, though thanks to the internet, I have been able to do most of that from my desk at home!

What I found out about Hannah More has made me more and more interested in her and keen to show young people what I have learned. She lived at a time like ours when it wasn't cool to be a Bible believing Christian; in fact she was often criticised for her faith. But God used this passionate, sometimes bossy, always very ambitious woman to change many people's lives for the good. We need more Hannah Mores today who will work hard and use their talents in God's service. Maybe you will be one of them!

The First School

The scraping of benches and stools and the bang, bang, banging of the door stopped. Hannah peeped her head round the door that connected the parlour and the school room.

'Yes, they've all gone, Hannah, you may come in,' said weary Mr More, who was sitting behind a high desk at the front of the simple classroom. Hannah grinned and turned her head to call.

'Come on, Patty! Sally, come on! We can play, they've all gone.' She rushed in, followed by a taller girl holding the hand of a smiling toddler. Hannah had dark eyes which seemed to flash with ideas and dark brown hair pulled back from her face. 'Patty, sit down and wait nicely,' said Hannah, as she and Sally began tugging and pushing the heavy benches and the few desks at which the thirty village children had sat. 'Our school will soon be ready!' Their father, fearing noise was ahead, quietly slipped from his high seat and went out of the far door towards the peace of his vegetable garden.

'Now, we're ready!' Sally stood on a bench, towering precariously over her two younger sisters who sat below her on the hard floor. 'The alphabet, if you please!' Hannah and Patty chanted the alphabet as loudly as they could before Hannah began to recite a poem. After this, Patty could sit still no longer and began to run in circles over the flag-stoned floor. Hannah and Sally straight away started to chase her and soon became dizzy, collapsing in giggles into each other's arms. 'What a school! Imagine if Father's boys behaved like this!' panted ten-year-old Sally as she started to race round again.

Hannah loved this time of the day, when she and her sisters could escape the confines of their cramped cottage and imagine they were at school like the farmers' sons that came every morning to learn reading and writing from her father. She couldn't understand why they moaned and grumbled about books whilst they ate their packages of bread and cheese. If only she could have lessons all day and not just by the fire in the evening! While the boys were sitting down with their slates she was helping her mother, scrubbing or mending or minding little Patty. Still, Hannah reckoned that she knew more than those clumsy boys and the few girls who were allowed to school too. They just learned enough to get by at market, whereas she had learned about Hector and Achilles, heroes and goddesses, adventures and wars.

'Hannah! Hannah! Carriages!' Two-year-old Patty had grown tired of running and wanted her favourite game.

'Alright dearie,' said Hannah , 'We'll play carriages. Sally, help me pull out this chair.' Over went the chair and Hannah sat on top of it with Patty on her knee. In her hands were the imaginary reins of a pair of smart black horses and the battered school room chair was a coach rushing towards London. Bounce, bounce, bounce went the giggling toddler and all the while Hannah kept up her commentary. 'Over the river and round the bend, mind the pothole, hold on! We're off to see the bookshops and buy ourselves some stories! We'll find you an Aesop's Fable, Patty, and I'll have some Plutarch in Latin, for Father's said I'd be able to read it – I'm taking to Latin so well. We'll buy Father all the books he lost and more besides!'

'What will mother have?' cried a breathless Sally. 'Shall we buy her poetry or sermons? And Mary and Betty? Let's buy them all books too! And let's visit the theatres and churches. I can see the dresses now, the big gowns and huge wigs! Hannah, can't you imagine them too?' The dull, brown school room became the dazzling streets of London as Sally and Hannah played and Patty listened, eyes wide as her sisters, described the gold, jewels and silks of their imaginations.

'Supper, girls!' Mother's kind face appeared from behind the door.

'Yes, oh quick, come on! Patty, go with Mother will you?' In a trice, Hannah and Sally became serious and started to work quickly. They pulled up the furniture and placed it ready for the morning's lessons and for the unwilling schoolchildren who would soon slouch in.

In the parlour, Jacob More was standing in front of the fire. At fifty-two he looked and felt like an old man; teaching was hard work and not the career he had dreamed of. When he was a boy, he'd been to a fine old grammar school where he had learned not only to write, but to speak in Latin. He'd studied ancient Greek and complicated mathematics. He'd had dreams of being a gentleman and not having to work. But all that had come to nothing. He had little money and a very small house. There was no genteel life for those who hadn't the right family connections.

He had worked for a while as a taxman, travelling around the countryside checking up on shopkeepers and farmers. But that had been a young man's job. His aching limbs weren't up to those long rides on horseback any longer. So he'd settled for this school. Every day twenty poor boys came to the school room to learn from him. They were good lads really; the sons of servants and farm labourers, who would end up as servants or farm workers themselves. They learned to read and write a little and how to add up and take away – just enough maths so they wouldn't be swindled at market. Ten girls came too and, alongside some reading, learned how to sew and spin from his wife, Mary.

'I just can't see how we can go on, Mary,' Jacob sighed. 'Hannah remembers everything and keeps talking about books. Her mathematics is better than the best of my oldest students and she is only eight! The lessons will have to stop!'

'Jacob! I can't believe you're speaking like this! Stop teaching her because she's learning too much?

Give up on her because she enjoys it too much? This is nonsense!' Mary turned to face her husband. She clattered the bowls down as loudly as she dared. Looking across at Patty who had started to whimper, she continued in a loud whisper. 'You loved your books and your studies. I never had the chance – all I had was my mother to teach me on the farm. And now you think you can take that opportunity away from our Hannah. The one you think is the brightest of the lot!'

'But if she carries on this way she'll never marry. A freak is what she'll become – a woman knowing more than any man. She'll be a laughing stock. No man will want her, and what will we do with her? No Mary, she needs to learn how to earn a living, not how to show off her learning.'

Mary More turned back to stir the stew cooking over the fire. No more lessons for Hannah? Round and round went her spoon. No more Latin or Maths, the subjects her own husband loved to teach?

'But Jacob, you will miss it so; those lessons are what you look forward to each day. Hannah could do so much more; you yourself say you've never taught anyone like her ... she could go to London and ...'

'Mary, you don't understand. An educated woman is like a dog walking on its hind legs – marvellous, but for the circus. No, I've made up my mind. No more boys' learning for Hannah. She can follow the others.' Mary More gritted her teeth and continued to stir. She had married Jacob when she was only seventeen. Only a year later, she'd had her first child. And now she had five girls, all of them busy and bright, but hard work! Of course she loved them to bits, each one of them so different from the others. And she didn't mind the darning and mending to keep clothes decent and the scrubbing and chopping to keep a meal on the table. But it all seemed so precarious. What if they didn't marry, or married a bad man? How could five girls find a way for themselves in this hard world?

Jacob got his way of course, though Mary didn't give up. Eight-year-old Hannah joined in with the sewing, the sweeping and the washing which went on week by week. She played with her sisters, imagining all kinds of new worlds and at night, after the school lessons stopped, Hannah still crept into the school room. In that room she could remember her lessons and pick up scraps of paper left by the boys. These she took care to hide in the broom cupboard where no one else could find them, writing her own stories on them and then squirrelling them away like nuts stored for winter. She didn't forget the Latin she had been taught and still curled up on her father's knee every night to hear about heroes like Odysseus and the monsters he fought. There weren't many girls in his stories though. All they seemed to do was wait, like patient Penelope, and Ariadne who got stranded on a beach. Women in the Bible stories her father read to the whole family seemed to have more interesting jobs. There she learned about Ruth who harvested, Lydia who was a merchant and clever Abigail who seemed to know just the right thing to do. Then there were the women who followed Jesus – they were pretty busy and important, quite like her mother, Hannah thought!

On a Sunday, the More family walked through the village to church. All the children from school were there, watching the school family arrive and sit still all through the long service. Week by week, Hannah looked at the communion table pushed back against the wall of the church. It seemed so very far away from their pew and the rector's words seemed very quiet as he repeated the words from the prayer book. The Ten Commandments written up in gold lettering on either side of the chancel were nearer and easier to understand; Hannah knew what these instructions meant and she knew that she had to try to obey them. And when she wasn't thinking about those words, her mind wandered to her own words, her stories and her games. Just like her mother, she thought and daydreamed about the day when she would be grown up. What would she do?

New Plans

A few months later, Hannah got a shock.

'Girls, quieten down! Sally, shush. Put down your spoon, Betty.' Mrs More looked round the crowded table. Five girls looked back. 'Your father has something to tell you, Mary.'

Mary, who was the eldest and named after her mother, and, Hannah thought, far too bossy, sat up straight and smiled across at her father. He coughed and looked down at his porridge.

'Yes, well, Mary, we've decided. That is, we have found a place for you. You see, it's time for you to add to your, erm, your accomplishments, to get ready for the world. We've found a school in Bristol … that will take you.'

Hannah and her sisters began to speak at once. Patty, not understanding what was happening, sucked her thumb harder.

'To teach?'

'No, to learn.'

'Mary is going to school? Then, why can't I?'

Hannah felt the resentment well up in her and she looked down into her bowl as if there she might find some answers. Patty, hearing the words 'Mary' and 'go away,' began to cry.

'Girls!' Their mother spoke sternly. 'Girls, calm yourselves. What you father is telling you is good news. We can't afford to send you all away to school. But we can send one of you, so Mary, as she is the oldest, will go every day to Bristol and every Friday she will teach you what she has learned. She will learn French. Because as you know, girls, we can't keep you here forever.'

Betty, who was twelve, joined Patty in crying.

'Go away? But mother, I don't ever want to leave. I like helping you here. I enjoy the sewing and cooking and being in the school room to help the little ones.'

'Oh Betty, this is a charity school. We won't have the money for your gowns and food as you all grow. And what can you do? Go out to be a servant? No, my love, what you do here, you wouldn't want to do in a stranger's house. If Mary learns to speak French prettily and teaches you all, you will be able to teach fine girls. Imagine that! A paying school with gentlemens' daughters; the More sisters, all teachers!'

Hannah lifted her head.

'So Latin is for boys, but French is for girls?' she asked glumly.

'Well, Hannah, boys can speak any language as you know, but girls, well French suits them best. At least, in society all the ladies speak French. Now, those boys will be here soon, so girls eat up!'

Hannah wasn't really satisfied with her mother's answer, but knew she shouldn't argue. At least she'd be learning something, and now she saw some light ahead. She knew that her parents were being very wise in seeking to equip her sisters and herself with a way to earn a living. And maybe, she thought to herself, maybe they really would make a success of a girls' school. At least that would be better than being a governess and living in a rich man's house, neither one of the servants nor one of the family.

And that was that. Mary went away to Bristol and every Friday night four eager students gathered round, Patty sitting on Hannah's knee and copying her sister's every word. As they learned French the girls also learned about Bristol. Although only five miles away from the two-bedroom cottage in which they lived, the city of Bristol was a magnificent new world to them, the second city in England and growing all the time.

'Down by the docks you see such sights.' Mary told them one Saturday as they all lay together in their one bedroom. 'Huge ships with rigging so high and the men scurrying up faster than you could run round the school room, Hannah. The sailors look like wild men when they come off-board. You should see the way they walk, and their skin! Browner than the farm boys in harvest! I'd never seen a colour like it until …' Mary stopped and looked around at their faces. 'Until this week, it was Wednesday after lessons, I saw a man from Africa, you know, not a sailor, but a native. He was as black as coal, and the hair under his hat was springy. Like coils of twisted wool.'

Hannah leaned forward onto the blanket, her elbows on her knees and chin in her hands.

'Was he fierce? What did he wear?'

'Oh no my love, not fierce!' Mary laughed. Hannah twisted her mouth. Mary had become even more big-sisterish and irritating since she had been sent to Bristol. 'Hannah, do you know nothing? No, the grand people like to have these Africans as servants – though they are not servants really – they don't get paid like our Martha does. They are slaves. That's what the ships are for. They leave Bristol to go and collect them from Africa and take them to America. Then the ships come back to Bristol full of sugar. Like a triangle – very neat! And some of the ship owners here like to have one of these slaves as a footman. They dress them up in velvet and lace so that folks stare. Showing off really … I suppose.'

'So the sugar is paid for with Africans? I wonder what the Africans think? Do you think they mind?' Hannah sat back on her heels and thought whilst Mary ignored her questions and continued.

'The sugar is interesting too. It doesn't come off the ships in twists of paper as mother sometimes buys.'

'She hardly ever does. Not enough money,' interrupted Sally glumly.

'No, they have to put it in great fires to cook it. You can see the chimneys and smoke all over the town, like dragons breathing fire.'

'Dragons sitting on gold!' interjected Sally.

'Well maybe, oh but the real gold is in the coffee houses. That's where the men with wigs and money are. We're not allowed to walk near there, of course,' Mary added primly.

Hannah's mind was set ablaze. This city seemed to promise so much; over the next six years she heard of ladies in ball gowns and men in high-heeled shoes, of tea parties where the talk was of politics and London and books. Mary had a clever knack of getting invited to some of these occasions and as she grew older, she sometimes took Betty and Sally along. Together they had got to know the right sort of people – ones who had daughters and money. Hannah couldn't wait to be there too and would lie in the bed she now shared with her sisters, making plans for the school they would share and of a life of fame beyond.

On the 12th of March, 1758, Mary arrived home breathless. She'd had a busy week in Bristol, and was now a very elegant lady, or at least Hannah thought so. But Mary didn't swan through the cottage door as she normally did. No, this time she rushed in, didn't take off her hat and grabbed thirteen-year-old Hannah by the waist. As they danced around the scrubbed table Mary sang. 'It's done, it's done, we're really on the way. The school, the school, we're in the paper today!' And with that she flung onto the table, narrowly missing a jug of milk, a fresh copy of the Bristol Journal.

'Look, Mother! Father, here we are, this page – can you see?' Patty had run in from the parlour, and Sally had leapt down the stairs. Hannah grabbed the paper from the table and read;

'At Trinity Street, near College Green on Monday after Easter will be opened a School for Young Ladies by Mary More and sisters ... Oh Mary, you've done it!'

'Read on, Hannah! That's not all! Read the words about the subjects!'

'Yes ... here we are "... will be carefully taught French, Reading, Writing, Arithmetic and Needlework." It's perfect, Mary! No Latin or Greek, but it's perfect! How did you do it?'

'My dear, you know I've no money. But Mrs Gwatkin, when I told her of our plans, said she'd lend us some to get us going, then there were others – so kind! But we've to make it work! Betty will teach with me, and you and Sally shall be our first pupils!'

The next few weeks were one long flurry of packing and practising. Dresses were altered and smartened up. Each one of the More sisters had to look the part for this new family business. Then the girls eagerly waited to see if any wealthy Bristol families would respond to the advertisement.

Drama!

The house behind the cathedral was solid and square with room for plenty of girls. Rooms filled up quickly as merchants and the nobility realised that this new school could provide a safe and respectable place for their daughters. With the headmistress being only nineteen and the matron seventeen, you can imagine that the school was not too serious a place, and yet it flourished. Patty, Sally and Hannah loved their lessons. Hannah was busy every day learning and talking and listening. She started learning Spanish and Italian from visiting teachers and kept up her French and Latin. Soon she was considered fit to teach and began to help with the little ones.

'Come on now girls, follow me, up the stairs and into the classroom. Miss More will instruct you in geography before the dancing master arrives.' Hannah ushered the twelve-year-olds into the room where they sat in front of her sister Mary. She stood at the back of the classroom watching out for misbehaviour whilst Mary lifted up the globe in her left hand and started to name the countries of the east. The girls began to repeat the names 'Siam, Ceylon …' but Hannah heard their whispers.

'I'm going to order a new muslin. My old one got torn yesterday and I can't be bothered to mend it. Mother will send the money, only I'll have to pretend that it is beyond repair. You know what these teachers are like about making do.'

'What will you say? Miss Patty saw you tear it.'

'I'll rip it tonight. I so want one with a new lace panel. Eliza has got one with that new style, you know, with the pink threaded through, and I can't let her seem more fashionable than me!'

'Of course not. She is such a pain, thinks she is better than anyone else, just because her aunt is a Duchess. We have to show her.'

Hannah didn't interrupt, but listened carefully to the two chatterers at the back until Mary glared at her. She pulled herself together and said sharply.

'You two, quiet now, or you'll miss your dancing.' The girls rolled their eyes, but fell silent.

Hannah couldn't stop thinking about what she'd heard. It wasn't a surprise. As a pupil and now as an assistant teacher, she'd heard so much sniping and jealously amongst the girls. She thought that she and her sisters had never behaved like this. With very little money they hadn't had a chance to worry about clothes and had always known they would have to work hard. Besides, their father's Bible stories had always reminded them that God would judge even their thoughts and secret conversations. That had been enough to stop

their little cruelties. She made up her mind to talk to
Mary and Betty later on.

'I'm just fed up with these petty battles between
the girls!' She burst out when finally the pupils were
settled and she could sit with her sisters in their tiny
parlour. 'It's not so much that they are mean; it is that
they are so vain! I know I was never like that when I
was their age!'

Mary smiled and Hannah continued. 'Why are
you smiling at Betty like that? Aren't you upset? Do
you think it is right that they care more about clothes
and hair powder than their lessons or other people?'
Hannah was warming up for a real rant but her oldest
sister stopped her.

'Hannah. First, you are only two or three years
older than these girls and second, are you not vain?'

'Me? Vain? What are you thinking of Mary? I'm ...
Oh Betty, you tell her.' She was starting to get upset,
so Betty stepped in.

Hannah's face fell. The five sisters could hear the
fire crackling but nothing else. All was still and all
waited to hear how the noisiest sister would respond.
Patty couldn't bear it, she stuttered.

'But Hannah, you are so clever, we all do think well
of you. What I mean to say, is that, well, we do all love
you, I don't think Mary meant any ...'

Hannah looked at her sweet youngest sister and
shook her head slowly. Patty's protestations petered
out.

'Mary, I think you are right. We're all ambitious, aren't we? There I was, looking down on those girls, when really I can be self-centred and a show-off too. I'm sorry, only I've been thinking about our pupils for a while. We have to have our feet on the ground, but these girls, they come from such wealthy families that they can live in these dream worlds, worrying about petticoats and powder or idling their lives away. That won't make them happy. So how can we help them? Lectures won't do any good. We need to excite their imaginations and inspire them to be better than those empty-headed ladies out there …'

'Now you're lecturing us! ' Mary laughed. 'We do agree Hannah, we don't need persuading! But maybe you're the one to do something about it.' Hannah went upstairs that night, determined to make a difference; perhaps attitudes could be changed and perhaps she had a way to do it.

The next few evenings, she was not to be found in the parlour with her sisters, instead she stayed in the school rooms alone, working at one of the girls' desks, quill in hand and dark eyes shining. Her sisters noticed she seemed tired in lessons, but they said nothing. On Saturday, they all went out for a trip to The Jacob's Well Theatre, the pupils walking in line with the sisters chaperoning and doing their best to look old and dignified. The theatre was in a rough part of town, and Hannah made sure she kept her eyes fixed on her pupils and away from the dirt and dust of her surroundings. Once in the theatre though, she couldn't hide her excitement. This was another world; it was her favourite place of all. The building was so small that actors had to walk out and round the back to be able to enter on the other side of the stage, and there was a hole in one wall right through to the next door pub so that the audience could order their drinks throughout the performance!

All sorts came to the theatre, from rich merchants and their wives to poor servants filling the pit next to the tiny stage. You could watch the changing fashions and the flirtations of Bristol before your very eyes, but Hannah was oblivious to that noise and display. She leant forwards in her seat, resting on the edge of the box high above the stage, ignoring the rowdy young men who were themselves ignoring *King Lear* on the stage. They were more interested in eating and laughing at some private jokes. Behind her, the Duchess's niece smirked and giggled, mimicking the actress sighing on stage, but Hannah was transfixed and, as the play drew near to its climax, tears rolled down her face. Shakespeare's words moved her deeply and she heard in them a promise of beauty and truth, far away from the squalor she had glimpsed on her way to the theatre.

Once out in the August air, Hannah spoke to her students about the play. Some, like the ones behind her, seemed uninterested. They commented on the clothes of the nobility who had been sitting next to them – laughing about the lady who was wearing such wide panniers on her hips that she'd taken up two seats. Those were so old-fashioned. Ladies in London, they'd heard, were dressing much more simply now. When Hannah tried to find out what they thought of the play, they groaned, 'Oh Miss More really! Must you? What a dull play. We saw *Love and Magic* last summer – now that was so much more exciting. I laughed so much I could have died! It was such fun. Or, what was that romance we saw called? You know the one where the bishop's daughter elopes with the butcher's boy …?'

Hannah gave up trying to explain the plot of *King Lear* and how it had plenty of shocks and horror, but they wouldn't listen, so she moved down the line to talk to much more sympathetic girls whom she knew would have enjoyed the play.

By the time the crocodile of schoolgirls and young school teachers had reached the new school building in Park Street, Hannah had recruited her first actresses. Those late nights in the school room had resulted in a play; not a comedy like *Love and Magic* or a romance full of immorality, but a play about wisdom.

She told Patty that evening, 'If I can't lecture my girls into wanting what's best, maybe we can persuade them through a story. I've written 'The Search for Happiness' to show them that fashion or fame or even knowledge itself won't bring them happiness. Proper religion will. Trusting in Christ is the only way they can be sure of satisfaction. Giving your life to him ... here is one way I express it:

'Fountain of being! Teach us to devote
To thee each purpose, action, word and thought!'

'What do you think? There are eight parts and it is all rhyming. Just a short thing really, but I think it might work. I've got Emily, Lydia, Betty and ...' Hannah barely paused for breath as she explained to Patty the arrangements for costumes and rehearsals. The next few weeks seemed just as breathless as these arrangements were carried out to the letter. Whether the girls heeded the lessons of the play or not, they loved the excitement of a theatre in their own school. Soon other schools heard of the play and were asking for copies. Hannah's reputation grew; she was the clever school mistress, the teenage play-writer, whilst week by week, month by month she kept on teaching. Was that it? She thought. She longed to write and to be free but you needed money for that! Sometimes she wondered whether, having been born in a school, she would stay in a school for the rest of her life.

Love Story

Belmont Park was huge. On top of a hill-like a fort, it allowed you to see to the River Severn far away and across to the Mendip Hills on the other side. In between house and hills, the grounds swept up and around and beyond, displaying soft green slopes and dark clusters of trees. In every direction there was something to charm the eye and Hannah certainly was charmed. She slipped her arm round Patty's waist as they waited on the terrace for their host, Mr William Turner. He had invited them and his cousins, their pupils, to spend a week with him, enjoying the country air and resting after the term at school. Hannah thought how she'd love to live in a place like this, in this newly built, orderly house, with tall windows, six on one side of the door and six on the other. But then, wasn't that every girl's dream? Or, at least, wasn't it the dream of every girl who had to worry about earning a living? This house seemed to breathe peace. Everything will be well, it said. All is in order.

The calm was broken by the girls running down the steps from the glazed front door. 'Miss Patty, Miss Hannah, we're ready! So sorry to keep you waiting!' Emily and Susannah were not much younger than

Patty and Hannah, but they were rich and so they could be pupils, not teachers. In the school holidays, when Patty and Hannah were helping their big sisters to prepare dormitories, Emily and Susannah could go to concerts and balls and could fuss over the latest fashions.

'Now, Miss Hannah, Cousin William said to meet him in the laurel grove. We must walk fast, he said, and look closely at the new trees he's planted along the avenue. Now, what are they called? Chestnuts? No, that's not it. Oh I don't know! Susannah, help me!'

Susannah shook her head and smiled at her teachers. 'I certainly can't remember anything. All these plants he's forever talking about are a mystery to me.' Patty and Hannah exchanged a glance. Susannah normally knew a lot more than she let on, but it was true: her interest certainly wasn't in plants, but in people. She looped her arm through Hannah's spare one and together they made their way down the path between the rows of young trees which stood to attention like boy soldiers. Hannah did look closely at the trees and noticed the brightness of their green leaves and the notches around the broad leaves. She breathed in deeply and smelt the scents of hay-making weather: dust, sweet hay and flowers just at their best. Nature seemed perfection. A poem began to form in her mind and she promised herself to write it as soon as she got back to the bedroom she and Patty were sharing.

William Turner was making promises too as he waited for the group of girls to meet him in the grove. He walked impatiently between the laurels and looked up to the path which wound down from the new avenue. He paced about and looked from tree to tree. Which one was growing best now? Where should he build the temple? How could he make the path seem more natural? Questions skittered in and out of his distracted mind, but again and again he returned to his promise. I will speak to Miss More today, he vowed. I will speak to her on her own.

The noise of the girls quickly brought William from his agitated thoughts and movements. He stood still and smiled as they came down the path. The three youngest were chattering together whilst Hannah was looking around her carefully as she walked.

'Welcome to my bower, Miss Hannah, and Miss Patty – oh yes, you too Susannah and Emily, but you've been here before, haven't you? You've seen how I felled some of these laurels to let in a bit more light. Now, what do you think – are the trees growing better?'

Emily and Susannah nodded cautiously. 'Yes, Cousin, yes, I suppose so … At least, whether they are or not, it does look pretty here,' offered Emily. She looked to Susannah for support. 'Oh yes, certainly it is very pretty.' She agreed. Hannah sighed.

'Girls, you aren't really looking properly, are you? Stand back here, where I am, and look.' Dutifully the three others moved to the edge of the path whilst Mr Turner hovered behind.

'Don't you see how that big laurel here obscures the view? We walk from the light of the path and enjoy the sun's rays falling from the east in the morning, but look to the west now.' All eyes turned to where Hannah pointed. There they saw two laurels close together in front of a gate into a copse.

'Move just one of those and the visitor will be drawn to explore the woods. You could open it out and … Oh please, excuse me, Mr Turner. I'm still teaching now, aren't I? On holiday and treating my host as a pupil? Forgive me.'

William looked flustered now. Hannah bowed her head and waited for him to say the right thing, to excuse and change the subject, perhaps to make a joke or display his gallantry. He was, after all, double her age and a rich man. Instead he blushed and began to stutter.

'Miss M-M-More, no I m-must do, I m-m-must, yes what you say is right, of course, the trees I think, they can, yes Miss M-M-More …What I mean to say …' He looked about to his cousins for aid but they seemed amused by something he did not understand. 'What I mean, Miss More, is that I am honoured.' He looked down and moved away from the group, appearing to be entranced by the bark of the laurel Hannah had pointed to. And so the girls began to talk amongst themselves. Susannah asked Patty a question, Hannah chipped in and they were back to their conversation, talking about books they had been reading and other girls at school. Mr Turner traced the rough cracks in the bark and looked up back towards the house. 'Shall we go?'

As the party walked into the house, Mr Turner turned to Hannah, 'Miss More, will you help me?' He paused and Hannah waited for him to continue. Her friends had drifted up the wide staircase. It was time to take off their day gowns and get dressed for dinner; Mr Turner had invited a neighbour and his daughters to dine, they would soon be arriving. 'I mean, will you help me with my plans, you see I'm concerned about the temple ...'

Hannah smiled. She had been unsure about Mr Turner all morning. Today, his kindness and confidence had vanished and had left a stuttering, blushing curiosity.

'Your temple? Oh, I see, in your garden, why of course, but you see now I must join Patty ...'

'Miss More, just one moment, if you would please look with me at the plans in the library now?'

Hannah was caught. Into the library she went, hoping that the plans wouldn't take too long. She had hoped to mend her rather old silk dress and make it presentable for another dinner.

But Hannah's thoughts were not on her dress when she came out of the library a quarter of an hour later, nor were they on temples or trees or any such things. She trod slowly and deliberately up the stairs repeating to herself 'Mrs Turner, Mrs William Turner … The Turners of Belmont!'

The remainder of the holiday was a whirlwind. Mr Turner and Hannah spent time discussing the garden and Hannah did offer good advice about the building of a temple in the grounds.

'Temples are quite the thing, you're right. Slender columns and a rounded roof to draw the mind to the classics and a bench for walkers to sit and regard the view. You must provide shelter too, I think; make sure the picturesque is also comfortable, Mr Turner, that would be perfect!' But no longer were the plans just for Mr Turner; this would soon be Hannah's home.

At night, Patty and Hannah talked and talked together until late as in the old days in their creaky school house bed.

'I am discovering more and more about William, Patty. He has a soft heart and wants so much to do good here. I can stand beside him and help him. And you will never be in need again. We'll make sure of that. Neither Mary, nor Betty, nor Sal will have to worry. And he wants me to write too; I'm not just to be a decorative wife he said, all tea parties and embroidery. I'll be able to write whatever I like Patty! I can't sleep tonight, it's too exciting!'

'And I'm excited too! You're the first of us all to become engaged, and you're only twenty-two;

how we'll miss you!' The sisters were making their
own plans. Not about gardens, but about school and
clothes. On the last day at Belmont, Hannah had made
up her mind.

'I'll be stopping teaching very soon, Patty. I've
written to Mary to let her know. It just wouldn't
be right to keep teaching when I'm engaged to a
wealthy man. You can manage without me and I can
concentrate on getting ready for the wedding!'

That getting ready meant shopping. Bristol was a
boom city where new shops were opening all the time
and suddenly Hannah was free from careful penny
pinching, mending clothes and making do. She took
her savings and spent much of them buying new silk
imported from overseas, finding patterns and being
measured by seamstresses whom she noticed treated
her differently now. To be William's wife, she must fit
into his gorgeous new house and be fit to mix with
those who had previously been employing her. She
felt like a character from a play, a Cinderella whom
good fortune had found out. The weeks rolled on with
Hannah able to enjoy her new independence, living
with her sisters but having no responsibility for the
school. She could socialise with her friends at the
theatre and in the city whilst dreaming of the beauty
of Belmont which awaited her.

Belmont was only six miles from Bristol and so
visits there were easy. Each time she visited, Hannah
could more easily imagine herself as Mrs Turner,

hosting gracious parties and settled as a fine lady, but at the same time she noticed that William's manner was growing more distant. As they walked through the grounds together, Hannah saw tiredness in his features. It was February by now and the ground was wet. Picking up her skirts and wrapping her shawl closely to her, she attempted to walk more briskly. At the edge of Belmont's grounds they stopped. Mist was spoiling the view of the Severn, but William wanted to carry on.

'There is something I must show you,' he said and led the sisters away from their usual path. 'Look!' he said pointing ahead. The women walked on ahead of him perplexed. The large boulder in front of them seemed dull. A misshapen column streaked with rusty red and orange.

'It's sandstone.' William explained. 'I call it my Bleeding Rock.' Hannah shivered. Her feet were getting very cold. 'Why bleeding? What a horrid name! Come William, let's go.'

'Bleeding because when it rains red water runs off the rock. Looks like its bleeding. Yes, we'll go.'

As they walked back, Hannah mulled over the rock. Rain as red as blood. It sounded like a fairy story or one of the Greek myths. Maybe a good idea for a story. When she was married she would write that story, she could come up to this strange rock in spring and write. Now, there was too much to plan and think about. The wedding breakfast for a start …

As they drew closer to the cedar walk, Hannah was jolted from her thoughts by William. His pace had grown slower and slower, he sighed from time to time and then stopped. As her own step stopped he looked at her and spoke in a rush.

'Hannah, m-m-my dearest, you know I esteem you very highly, I admire you to the utmost. But, my dear, I fear that we m-m-must postpone the wedding.'

Escape to London

Hannah had noticed her fiancé's silences and his nervousness many times before, but then she knew he was an older man, thoughtful like her own father, prone to introspection and pessimism. When we're married, Hannah had thought, I'll be able to cheer him out of these sombre moods. When we're married ... that phrase had seemed so exciting. Now it had turned into a question: when will we be married?

That question hung in the air for five more years. Five years, in which wedding plans were made again twice, and twice again William Turner postponed them. Hannah could feel the eyes of her friends and acquaintances on her as she went to the theatre and took tea. She couldn't go back to teaching as she'd renounced her share in the school; she was spending her life waiting for a wedding, her trunk of new clothes unworn in the corner. Now she was no longer a Cinderella, she'd become a laughing stock. Money was running out and all around her people were wondering why William Turner wouldn't get round to marrying her. Was something wrong with her? All she could do was wait, clinging onto the hope that her rich fiancé would finally stir himself out of his depression and marry her.

In the end, it was her sisters who came to the rescue. They called upon a vicar friend to talk to Mr Turner, and eventually the engagement came to an end. William offered to give her £200 a year which would mean that she no longer had any need to work – she had become rich at last, though not as she expected. Now, for the first time in her life, she was free to do as she pleased. Patty was delighted and wrote to a friend, 'this poet of ours is taken care of and may sit on her large behind and read, to devour, as many books as she pleases!' Hannah was less than delighted, though. Her heart had been wounded and she felt ashamed; through the last year of her engagement, she had been made ill with the strain of it all. And so now what was she to do?

London was the answer, the place of publishers and playhouses, the famous and the infamous. By travelling there she could extend her own writing success and also escape the stain of being unsuccessful in marriage. Already, Hannah was getting some attention for writing her poem-play, *The Search after Happiness*. It had been published in Bristol and many schools were performing it. She had other plans too: she had written a play called *The Inflexible Captive* that year and had ideas for more.

What a crowded place London was, thought Hannah as she travelled there with Patty and Sally. They were sore and tired after the two days in a jerky, jolting coach, luggage strapped to the roof and strangers riding beside them. They had been used to the strange sights of Bristol, but London seemed so much more exotic. With getting on for a million inhabitants, London dwarfed Bristol. The West End was full of tall new houses terraced together around small green parks. There were colonnades of shops too, selling all manner of hats and dresses, furniture and china. Carriages raced by on the uneven roads and an occasional sedan chair was carried through the mud by footmen dressed up in grand uniforms. In between these wove boys selling pies from trays hanging round their necks and women pushing carts and carrying baskets towards the great market in Covent Garden. There were others too; dirty, scruffy children, and women with bright makeup on their faces, lounging in doorways. The busyness matched her own racing heart. Here was a city she could start again in and find a new life.

Once in their rented rooms, the sisters began to plan.

'Mr Garrick has read my playscript once and turned it down, but I have high hopes. Reverend Stonehouse will surely persuade him to visit us, and Mrs Gwatkin has written to Sir Joshua the great painter – maybe there is an opening there …,' began Hannah.

'Slow down, Hannah! You mustn't run ahead. You'll wear yourself out again! Patty and I know we're here for your writing, but let's enjoy ourselves first. What about the museum? And the pleasure gardens? We have lots to see. We're tourists here after all!' Sally warned.

'Well, yes. Those places would be fun, but if we are to be pleasing ourselves, shouldn't we start with the theatre? Garrick is King Lear this week at Covent Garden!'

'Hannah, slow down!' interrupted Patty. 'I know the theatre isn't just another sight to see for you – it is business as well! Yes, of course we must go to Covent Garden. But promise me we'll be able to go to the gardens please. Let me have my fun too!'

Laughing together they managed to negotiate an itinerary, and so, within a few days the sisters had been to the most famous theatre in London to see the most famous actor in the world. David Garrick, actor, theatre-manager and playwright. Garrick almost was theatre! Hannah was overwhelmed.

Sitting down in their tiny sitting room she leant back in her chair.

'Patty, I feel I must describe my experiences, or they will be lost. Now, where is my writing case?' She lifted up a pile of books and found the neat wooden box. Opening it out, a slope was formed on which she could rest her paper.

'Every faculty of my soul was swallowed up in attention! Yes, that will do,' she said as she began a letter to friends back in Bristol. 'I was rapt and swooned – what do you think Patty? A bit much?' Hannah wasn't really waiting for Patty's replies; she was off in her own world, reliving the experience of seeing Garrick. She worshipped the great man and knew that if she was going to succeed in writing, she had to have his help.

'An invitation!' The sisters had been settled in their rented rooms for just a few weeks when the letter arrived. 'Please, Patty, open it!' Hannah begged, resisting the urge to snatch the paper from her sister's hands. 'Tell me what it says! Is it from him? ... I knew it!' she gasped.

Patty read out the invitation, 'Mr and Mrs David Garrick request the pleasure of your company ...' Hannah, he says we should wait for his carriage! Think of that – we're not to cross the street and walk there, but will travel like grand ladies in his carriage. Now, what should we wear?'

The three of them could hardly wait for the hour to arrive and when it did, the event far surpassed their expectations. The Garrick house was huge, with twenty-four elegant rooms, a pillared hall and a vast marble fireplace. For once, the women were stunned into shyness. They needn't have worried. Mr Garrick swept them into his home with real warmth. He played the part of host excellently and decided to take these three school teachers to his heart. Over the weeks, he introduced them to MPs, artists and writers. Hannah made a great impression on everyone she met. Dr Johnson, the most famous writer in London, learned one of her poems by heart and decided that she was the best female poet he had ever met! Better than everything else, Hannah found herself taken under David Garrick's wing. He and his wife had never had children and it was as if they adopted Hannah as their daughter. Patty and Sally travelled back to Bristol and teaching whilst Hannah remained in London, the permanent guest of the Garricks. She had arrived!

Only a year later, Hannah found herself on the other side of a stage. She paced up and down anxiously, amongst huge baskets of costumes and the clutter of props whilst actors and actresses muttered lines to themselves and performed strange exercises to warm up for the play. And this was no ordinary play; this was her play! The script which Garrick had turned down once, had now been accepted. It was a tragedy called *The Inflexible Captive,* based on a Latin story of nobility, honour and sacrifice. And now, in the fashionable town of Bath, her play was being performed by real actors in a real theatre! This was what Hannah had longed for.

As the performance was about to begin, she took her seat on the front row and watched with satisfaction as the audience around her fell silent. Grand ladies, with their wide skirts and tiny waists, in bright silks like so many butterflies, men in embroidered waistcoats and wigs all leant forward to see her creation. By half way through, the lady next to her was weeping, tears streaking her powdered face. Someone in the row in front, gasped at the noble hero's words and in the interval she could hear buzzing conversations all about her characters and her story. It was a success! People were being shocked and moved and stirred by the story she had written, perhaps they were even being inspired to live better lives!

'But the play isn't the only thing.' Hannah went on. 'Did you not see the poems I've recently published?' The tall woman shook her head. She was wearing a turban which seemed to make her even taller, and she towered over Hannah's short, plump frame. Hannah continued.

'Oh, they're silly things really, but my publisher seemed to like them. The next work I'm to publish will be much more serious however, and I must become a school ma'am again!' Hannah was standing in a large room in which groups of ladies were gathered, all talking energetically at once. Some were artists, some scholars, others just rich and interested. Hannah wondered what her father would have made of it all! A room full of educated, intelligent women!

'Tell me what it is Miss More. Another tragedy? A work of philosophy perhaps? I think the public will buy anything with your name on it!'

'You flatter me! I'm sure they wouldn't! It is a book of advice for young ladies on how to behave. I have seen a lot of young ladies behave badly ...'

'And you think that they will buy your book?' Her new friend interrupted with astonishment.

Hannah laughed. 'Well, they won't, but their parents will. Since I've spent so much of my life in schools, I've seen how many children don't care for education. But if they will start to care, then maybe we will have fewer problems in society. We need more religion and more respect! I intend ...'

The tall woman looked unconvinced, but at that moment Sir Joshua Reynolds came up, breaking up the conversation to ask if Hannah would consider sitting for a portrait with some of the other female writers and thinkers at the party. What an accolade! Hannah to be painted by the royal artist! She readily agreed and went quickly to tell Mrs Garrick the good news.

These years of fame passed in a blur. Hannah wrote and talked and read and went to numberless parties where she was known for her wit and her morals. She was proud of her reputation and enjoyed her fame. For a time, it seemed that she could achieve all she wanted, but five years after her first arrival in London her world began to tumble down.

'Did you hear what Johnson said the other day?' David Garrick had thrown a party and two of the men were sitting round a table, drinks in hand.

'He's always saying one thing or another to cause a scandal! Do tell me!' The gentlemen put their heads together to whisper then loud laughter rang out.

'Surely not! Hannah More she's one of his favourites, always by his side, flattering him and leaning on his arm.'

'That is the problem. A flatterer he said, and no elegance at all. He says the same as Boswell: ten out of ten for goodness but zero for appearance and manners!'

'I can't help but feel sorry for her though, did you see those reviews …'

The men suddenly hushed as a pair of smartly dressed women passed by, but it was too late. The cruel comments had been heard, and it didn't take long for them to reach Hannah's ears. The world she had pinned her hopes on was proving to be harsh and untrustworthy. It had welcomed her in, but was starting to turn its back on her. Worse still, David Garrick, her loyal protector, was seriously ill.

A New Book

Black carriages filled the street outside Westminster Abbey. Black plumed horses lifted their hooves and shied as crowds jostled to get a closer view of the celebrities who emerged from their carriages, swathed in clothes of mourning. What a spectacle! Hannah and Patty had never seen the like; nobles and actors jumbled together as each one pushed for the best seats at the front of the Abbey. This was David Garrick's funeral and it seemed the best drama in London. Inside the Abbey, Hannah and Patty felt hollow despite the hullabaloo. Garrick wasn't just a star to them; he was a friend. He had guided Hannah, advised her, given her a home and friends and now she felt as if she was on her own. How could she manage? Who would support her writing and protect her from the unkind critics and gossip-mongers?

Now stop it, she told herself and shook her head. *No more tears just now*. Taking Patty's hand, Hannah stepped forwards.

'We must get to some good seats, I want to hear and see well. Let's see if we can get in front of all these people here.' She pulled Patty through an imposing looking door.

'I think through here will take us up to a good vantage point. Come on, keep up!' Up the spiral staircase they went, and then, seeing another door, Hannah tried it. The room they entered was a store room, not a balcony or viewing gallery.

'Oh Hannah, this has been wild goose chase! Let's get back downstairs right away, we do need to find seats, we have got tickets after all.' But, just as Patty said those very words, the door slammed shut. Hannah tried the heavy metal handle but it wouldn't turn.

The two sisters looked at one another. Sealed off from the chatter of thronging crowds beneath, here there was an eerie silence. Patty looked as if she might cry again.

'I'm sorry,' said Hannah, 'I am really sorry.' She looked at the dusty chests that stood against the walls, an elaborate candlestick half covered in a grimy sheet and her sister's distressed face. Then she started to giggle. 'We're like the princes in the tower, or some damsels from a legend! What would old Garrick have made of this? Imagine how it would be on stage!' Patty's face crumpled; was she going to burst into tears? No, laughter spilled out.

'Hannah, what have you done? This is ridiculous! Serves you right for trying to be too clever! We must shout, maybe a verger will hear us?' The sisters bawled as loudly as they could for a few minutes, but their cries just bounced off the thick stone walls; no response. They sat down on the wooden floorboards. Patty sighed.

'This is so strange; here we are stuck in an Abbey tower whilst all the world is downstairs. I don't know why I don't feel terrified, but I don't, in fact it is almost a treat, being removed from all that hysteria downstairs. Still, someone is bound to come and rescue us eventually. Why don't we play a game while we wait?' And so they did, alternating twenty questions with calling for help. Patty was right, someone did come and they managed to see more than half of the funeral. Their strange incarceration had put them in a strangely cheerful mood despite the funeral.

That mood didn't last long, though. Once the funeral was over, Hannah sank into illness and depression. A holiday in the fashionable spa town Bath helped a bit, and the kindness of her friends and family was a comfort. But, without Garrick, she had started to question what on earth she was doing in London. She finished her most recent play whilst in Bath and handed it over to a publisher, but knew in her heart that it wouldn't be successful. A friend, seeing how ill and sad Hannah looked, gave her a new book to read.

She settled into her sofa and opened the first page, breathing in the delicious smell of new pages. The title page said *Cardiphonia*; Hannah knew that meant 'cries of the heart'. She'd read books about feelings and passion and she'd also read books about religion, but the two didn't really go together, she thought. She rubbed her forehead wearily and started reading.

It was a couple of hours later when Hannah put the book down. She'd been completely absorbed. *Well I never ...* she said to herself and then, smoothing her skirt, she got up from the sofa and nearly ran out of the room.

'Patty,' she called, 'Patty, where are you?'

In the corridor she met a tousled-looking Patty, whom she'd just woken from a nap.

'Hannah, what is it? Are you feeling worse? Do sit down, you're not better yet!' Patty bustled about her and wasn't satisfied until Hannah had been seated back down on the sofa.

'I can look after myself, sister! I'm not ill, just excited. Let me tell you about this book!'

'Oh, Hannah! A book? I thought it must be something important!' Patty teased.

'Dear sister, let me finish. Frances sent me this book.' Hannah lifted up the clothbound edition of *Cardiphonia*. 'It is extraordinary. Have you heard about that sea captain, vicar?'

'You mean the slave trader? John Newton's his name, isn't it? Go on.'

'Oh, this book isn't about him, it's about God! Listen, let me read you something from the beginning, I've copied it out into my notebook as it's so striking. "The Lord ... returns to convince, humble, pardon, comfort, and renew the soul. And thus we learn to tread more warily, to trust less to our own strength, to have lower thoughts of ourselves, and higher thoughts of him." What do you think of that?'

Patty began to smile. She began to understand why her sister was so excited. 'Higher thoughts of him? He means Jesus?'

'Yes, Patty, of course!' Hannah laughed. 'I have been full of thoughts of myself, haven't I? And now this wonderful book has forced me to think about our Lord. I've always been trying to serve him, but not for him; instead for me, so that I would look good. I've been so foolish!'

Hannah went on to explain to Patty what she'd discovered in the last two hours. 'You see, I always thought I just had to do my best and be as good as I possibly could be, or at least, be better than the others. But, well, I knew deep down that wasn't good enough; I could always have been better, or maybe I should have been better. Am I making any sense, Patty? My head is in a spin!' Patty nodded her head and Hannah continued, 'Whilst I was reading, it was as if he was writing just about me! He says, Patty, that even our best deeds are spoilt by sin, but that God forgives, not because we're good, but because Jesus died for us.'

Patty truly didn't know whether her sister was feverish or going mad. She'd never seen excitement like this during the reading of a religious book. People did warn against the silly enthusiasms of those people who followed preachers like John Newton and the Wesley brothers. She'd heard about them; they set up their own societies and didn't follow the Church of England rules. They held great big meetings in fields and all the rough miners and mill workers turned out to listen. All of it sounded very dangerous and wild. What was her sister getting mixed up in now?

In the weeks and months that followed, Hannah's life began to change. On the outside, not much was different. Hannah continued to write letters, to read, to visit friends and go to parties. But underneath, she began to look at her old habits with new eyes. Hannah had always believed that the Bible was God's Word and she had known the Creed and Catechism well. She had friends who had talked to her of Jesus Christ before, but now she had really begun to listen. Maybe the Methodists weren't bad, she reflected; after all they were preaching the message of forgiveness and new life that she was discovering for herself. She sat at her writing desk, her plump hand splattered with ink and her paper covered with crossings outs and blots, and wrestled with what to write.

Outside her window, she saw the wealthy and glamorous hurrying in carriages to the theatre. They were off to see Sheridan's latest play about a scandal. Yet all around them, in the streets thick with dirt and mud were walking scandals. There were barefoot women dressed in bright clothes fighting for the attention of men whilst children in grey rags begged. There were swindlers and cheats and soldiers and workers. Why have I never really noticed all this before, wondered Hannah. I've been blind to all this pain and sin. I don't want to distract people from what is going on around them. I know I can make an audience weep or laugh or clap, but what good will that do? When they walk out of the theatre there will still be little children begging.

Hannah turned back to her desk. Inside, everything was in its right place; the beautiful rich curtains, the pictures, the soft carpet. And when she looked in the mirror hanging above the fireplace she saw herself, a plump woman with dark eyes and hair fashionably mounded up high on her head, wearing a respectable blue dress with a clean white scarf round her neck. What could she do about the mess outside the window? What could she write or say that would make any difference? Now her eyes were open to what the Bible had to say about life, Hannah didn't want to write plays to make comfortable people weep or laugh, instead, she wanted to change people's hearts. She bowed her head to pray.

'Frances!' she said, turning to her hostess, an elegant older lady dressed in a fashionable silver gown. 'Frances, I have started to write again.' The eyes of Frances' guests turned upon her and Hannah realised that she had the full attention of the room.

'I was inspired to write by the book you leant me, and I'm working on a series of plays.' At this, the women and few men gathered for tea turned to each other and smiled, a few conversations began. All were intrigued that Hannah had started to write again. She was the best known female playwright in London, but her plays recently had not been successful and secretly some worried that she was losing her interest or even her skill, now that Garrick had died. Frances Boscawen, however, knew what the book she'd leant was, and so was ready for Hannah's news.

'I've not written a tragedy or a romance or even a comedy. My plays are called *Sacred Dramas*; there's a story about a baby in bulrushes and a story about a shepherd and a giant ...' Frances couldn't help interrupting

'You've made Bible stories into plays? Oh you clever thing! Will you show me them?' But whilst Frances Boscawen was delighted, other friends were less impressed and the conversations around the room became full of unpleasant whispers about Hannah.

'Of course, the stories are with my publishers at the moment, but you will be the first to see them, and I must tell you, I've written a poem for you which they'll be happy to print in the same edition. They don't know how many they'll be printing at the moment though, the publisher has always been so kind to me, but when I visited his office last Tuesday he laughed at me. He said that I was too good a person now to be a writer!'

The publisher was proved wrong. Hannah's *Sacred Dramas* sold like hot cakes. People who would never have gone to the theatre bought them and the plays were put on in homes and schools across the country.

But, despite the success, her friends now knew that Hannah had changed for good. The things that had once delighted her now bored her. Her friend, Samuel Johnson, had said, 'when you're tired of London, you are tired of life,' and Hannah was tired of London and she was tired of London life too. There was a constant temptation to gossip and to waste time talking about nonsense. Then there was all the suffering which made her feel so upset. 'If I can only be free from the city, then I will be so much better!' she said to Patty on a visit back to Bristol. 'You must help me hunt for a house of my own, away from the dirt and smells of this place. Let's go together back home, to the countryside, where the air is clean.'

Trying Hard

Hannah sat in the morning sunshine in Mrs. Garrick's breakfast room. In amongst the letters from builders, land-agents and carpenters, was a letter from Bristol.

'My Dear Sister,' wrote Mary. 'You will be astonished to hear of the woman who comes to our school kitchen to take away the scraps of food. Perhaps with your smart London life you've forgotten all about the pig-buckets and left over porridge in our busy kitchen here! But they are still here, and we've found a poet to take them away!' Hannah laughed out loud. A lady poet and pig food! This was oh-so-serious-Mary writing, so it must be true, but how extraordinary! She read on rapidly, scanning the lines to see how the story ended. When she had finished she folded the letter carefully and frowned. It wasn't such a happy story after all.

Ann Yearsley, for that was her name, had a horrid life, for all that Hannah could make out. She was only young, but married to a failed farmer and had lived with her five children in a stable. Now, with a bit of help from some wealthy friends, she was working as a milk-woman, delivering milk to, among other places, the More sisters' school. She took away the slops to feed to her pigs, but had left behind some poems that she had written.

'I must meet her, this rough poet,' wrote back Hannah to Mary. 'Will you arrange it for me? I think I can really help her!'

They met that summer at the school. Hannah was in her silk and Ann in her working clothes, sitting together on the drawing room sofa. Hannah was the one who looked the most flustered, though. Ann was calm, and even business-like.

'I used to read the books my ma brought home – she was a maid and her master let her take some to borrow. Virgil, the Latin one, was the one I liked best. All about nature and love were his poems. So that's how I try to write, when I write my poems.'

'And have you seen a dictionary, or a grammar book?' asked Hannah.

'No, I never have. I just write what seems right. Now, may I go?' Ann answered simply. She was wondering what this posh lady wanted with her. She had business to do, and money to make and felt as though she were being poked and prodded by a doctor.

Hannah was thinking about money too as she asked those questions. But in a different way. When Ann had gone, she rushed into Mary's room.

'Mary, I think I can help that poor woman! Her poems are good, and she has perfect taste. She just hasn't got the friends and contacts – well not yet, anyway! And that is how I can help. I know plenty of people – we can raise money and get her poems printed and then she'll be properly appreciated. I might start writing letters now. Can you lend me some paper?'

'Oh, Hannah! Sit down, and slow down!' Mary pulled up a chair for her sister, but it was no good. Hannah paced back and forth. 'No, I won't sit down here – I'll go to my room and write there. Mrs Montagu is the one to help I'm sure. We'll raise the money between us – we won't take her away from her family or try to make her something she's not ...' And with those thoughts, Hannah made for the stairs, humming to herself.

Mary sighed and pushed the chair back to where it had stood all along. *My sister's a whirlwind!* she said to herself. *I hope she is careful. Arranging other people's lives is dangerous business.*

But Hannah had more to occupy her than making Ann Yearsley into a poetry star. The plan to move out of London was at the front of her mind. She had never had her own home but had moved from her sisters' school to the homes of kind friends or rented rooms, and, just as she was tired of theatre life in London, she was also tired of her mobile life outside it. She had spent lots of time in Somerset visiting friends and that was where she planned to settle – it was near her sisters and parents in Bristol and out of the way of the fashion and gossip of London. *If only I had my own little hermitage, where I could pray and be at peace*, she told herself. *I'm sure I would be a better person.* And so she started to search.

There were some beautiful plots of land to choose from, some in the hills, some by streams. And Hannah chose well. Cowslip Green had a stream tumbling through and plenty of beautiful trees to spread their shadow on hot days. It was easy for Hannah to imagine her country cottage there; it was to look picturesque, as if it had always been there. She sketched pictures of the neat, thatched home she wanted and took them to show her London friends who cooed over them, though they themselves would certainly not have liked to live in such a tiny place.

The builders got on with their work quickly, and before long the cottage was up. It was perfect! Hannah was thrilled to be a homeowner at last and, more especially, to be a garden owner. Ever since she had helped William Turner plan his own magnificent estate, she had longed to have her own plot to cultivate.

'How blessed I am!' she thought as she knelt beside a very stubborn clump of nettles. It was an early August morning and the sun was just starting to get hot; soon she would have to retreat indoors, because she couldn't risk sunburn – only the farm workers did that. As she worked, a rabbit scurried from one fresh clump of grass to another and overhead a swallow was swooping in the blue sky. 'I couldn't be anywhere better! At last I am free to live a quiet life; I can write and do my good deeds and please God here far better than I could in London. Surely here I'll be able to concentrate when I pray. In London there were so many distractions.' She tugged at the nettle root and all of a sudden it came loose, throwing her off balance. Hannah laughed at herself and wiped her face with a rather grimy hand. 'Now, I think I'm free at last!' She threw the nettle in an old tin pail and moved across to the next patch. This was where she planned to plant tulips and irises to flower next spring. She was already looking forward to sitting on the lawn here, where at the moment it was so rough, and smelling the early flowers whilst she read. Of course, she would have visitors, and they would be amazed at her hard work. She could imagine now what fashionable Mr Walpole might say about her hermitage! Not only the summer sun, but the prospect of all that approval made her feel quite warm. Behind her, the cottage with its low thatched roof looked snug and inviting. One more weed, she promised herself before taking a rest inside.

It was just at that point that the postboy came, carrying letters from the nearby town of Wrington, and so Hannah found that her rest was interrupted by more than a nettle sting. Discarding the chatty note from her mother in Bristol, she opened the one with handwriting she immediately recognised. It was from Ann Yearsley and she was in debt and asking for money. 'I suppose I had better go and meet her.' Hannah said gloomily to her maid. It felt as though the sun had gone in.

A couple of days later, Hannah managed to meet Ann at her sisters' school. They all sat down for dinner together around the smooth oak table. Ann looked smarter than last time with a gold pin upon a neat dress. 'She has become very fine very quickly!' thought Hannah to herself as she tucked into the boiled beef. 'But she looks uncomfortable!' Once they had eaten, Hannah handed over the £10 Ann owed to a collection of shopkeepers and her landlord, saying, 'I can do no more. The money I've raised for you is tied up in a trust. Only Mrs Montagu or I can release it. And we put it there to keep it safe, so that it is not wasted, but saved for your children.'

Ann Yearsley's face went red.

'Wasted? What do you mean wasted? Do you think that I am not capable of spending money wisely?' Hannah shifted in her chair whilst Ann continued, 'Can I not see a copy of this deed to make sure you're telling the truth?' Hannah breathed in and out before she replied, trying to control her anger. 'Do you doubt my word? Perhaps you have taken too much wine and have gone mad and don't know what you are saying!' It was years since Hannah had been spoken to like this and she was furious. Ann Yearsley should have been grateful for her help, not doubting! And why did she want so much money? Quiet Betty tried to calm things down, but neither Ann nor Hannah were in a mood for reasoning. Ann left the house shortly after and Hannah retired to her bed to think.

'I simply can't understand her!' said Hannah a few weeks later to Mrs Montagu. 'I've done so much for her – I've even nearly sorted out a job for her husband.

She's argued with me about money and now she is criticising me in public — saying that I'm controlling her and exaggerating her story so that I look good!' She started to cry. 'I'm just trying my best. I wanted to help her and change myself. This was all part of my fresh start. I was leaving the arguments and foolishness of London behind, but now look! I've got my lovely country cottage, but there are still plenty of battles here!' Mrs Montagu did her best to soothe Hannah and offered her a lace-edged handkerchief to dry her hot tears. Together, they worked out a way to hand over the money to someone else to look after, and decided to leave Ann to her own devices. She was now a successful writer and business woman, dressing like a lady and with plenty of people interested in her. There was nothing more for Hannah to do.

Hannah had only wanted the best, but it hadn't worked out well. She had learned a few lessons herself though. It was hard to help people; sometimes they weren't grateful and sometimes they didn't even want help! As she spent more time at her hermitage, praying, reading and gardening, she wrestled with all that had happened. Her next project to help people would be very different.

Changing the World

'Yes, tea, please, Margaret,' replied Hannah as she sat in her friend's garden. Not quite as lovely as her own, she thought, but definitely more grand. The roses were of a very delicate colour and their scent drifted across the lawn. Behind them the great house rose up, looking like a temple, white and serene. She took a ladylike sip from the steaming cup.

'Ugghh! Oh, please, I do beg your pardon. I still can't quite get used to it without sugar, I'm afraid!' Hannah blushed. She did have a sweet tooth and, although she approved of Margaret's refusal to use sugar, it did make tea rather bitter.

'But Hannah, you must think of the slaves, then you'll not find it so distasteful. I never allow it in my tea. My protest can do very little, but it allows me to shock my guests, do you see? Then I can tell them the true cost of sugar; about how much the African slaves suffer.'

'A clever strategy, Margaret; I'm sure more and more people are coming to their senses about slavery. I don't really know of anyone amongst my friends who approves of stealing Africans from their homes and dragging them across oceans to produce our sugar.

But the trade goes on because there's so much money to be made.'

It was Lady Margaret who had described to Hannah the cruelty of the long journey, how the slaves were chained so closely together, with no light and hardly any air for a voyage eight weeks long across the Atlantic Ocean. Her husband was a Navy captain and he'd seen the suffering at first hand. Hannah had, of course, already known something of slavery from living in Bristol. She'd seen ships packed with cheap fabric, rum and even guns, ready to exchange for Africans. And she'd seen the sugar being returned from the Americas on the quayside – the end product of the trade. But that had seemed such an everyday part of life, a part of life which had made Bristol the rich and comfortable city it now was, that Hannah and her sisters had hardly thought of opposing it.

'Oh Hannah, how can you say nothing can change? God hates injustice and cruelty. He will help us. He is more powerful than all those rich traders and ship-owners and politicians.' Hannah smiled at her earnest friend. Of course Lady Margaret was right. Once Hannah had seen her own failures with Ann Yearsley, she had begun to realise how helpless she was to help even one person successfully. But the more time she spent with Lady Margaret and listening to sermons, the more she had become convinced that in God's strength she could do good.

'Margaret, I deserve that rebuke. I know God is powerful. My question is; what should I do?'

The two women talked about this for the rest of that afternoon. There was much for both of them to do. As women they couldn't stand up and argue in Parliament, but they could influence those who did. They couldn't even vote in elections, but they could persuade the men who did. So, both set about planning to change the opinions of a nation.

Lady Margaret's plan was to gather a group of men who could take the battle against slavery into parliament. She and Hannah could support the work, canvassing opinion and encouraging others to act. And so over the next year Hannah was often at Teston, sitting around the long dining table or in the library in front of a fire, talking and writing. There she met many people who would become her closest friends. What a relief it was to spend time with serious people who cared, like her, for the Lord and for his Kingdom – how different from the shallow, vain world of the theatre!

'Miss More, I am delighted to meet you! I have heard so much about you from our friend, Mr Newton. My name is William Wilberforce.'

'Well, I am delighted too, Mr Wilberforce. I hear that we've both got a great deal in common. Lady Margaret tells me that she has dragooned you to our side.' Hannah smiled, thrilled to meet this famous man, best friend of William Pitt, the young Prime Minister. She looked him up and down. Bright eyes, a slight frame and not much taller than she was. He hardly looked the type to take on the might of the ship-owning traders.

'You're thinking that I hardly look the fighting type! I can see it!' He laughed. 'Don't deny it Miss More. You see I often think the same, but then I remember God calling David, and Gideon and all those other weak vessels, and using them to bring victory. What is more, I know that I stand on the shoulders of these good folk here – Clarkson and Sharpe and the Middletons and all the myriad of others. I believe that we are working together, and best of all, the Lord walks with us. You know, as I was crossing the Thames at Westminster, I was meditating on Psalm 119.' Here, William grasped her arm and leant close. 'I was astonished afresh. It is the Lord who gives us wisdom; His Word is a light to our feet, is it not? So we needn't be afraid and downcast. He cares for these slaves more than we do!' Hannah looked up and saw that the whole room was entranced. All were gazing at this passionate man.

'You are right, Mr Wilberforce. When you speak in Parliament, I am sure that everyone will listen. And we will win freedom for the slaves.' They smiled at each other, understanding each other completely.

William Wilberforce was like Hannah in many ways. He had loved the grand society of eighteenth-century London too, though it hadn't been plays for him, but drinking and gambling which had occupied his heart. The old slave captain turned preacher, John Newton, who had challenged Hannah and gently led her to trust Christ only, had challenged William too. And now both were here, passionate in their new faith, keen to see the world changed.

'You must help me with my speeches, Miss More! You can see that I'm hardly ever lost for words, but perhaps I need more finesse. I hear that you're a grand writer and teacher; I'm sure you can improve them.'

'If you will be a good pupil, I'll be glad to help. But to me you look a little mischievous; I think you might not sit still!' They both laughed and then William continued.

'That is true, very true. I do try hard though; the problem is that there is so very much to do! But tell me about how you will serve the cause? Your talents are in writing, why don't you write a play or poem to stir the hearts of men? I can address a few hundred in parliament; you can address thousands in print.' The two settled into chairs a little away from the fire and the ears of the others who were standing and sitting in Lady Middleton's high-ceilinged drawing room.

'Now I feel more comfortable.' William leant back in his chair. 'This whole house is an extraordinary place. Don't you feel that too?' Hannah looked around her. There was James Ramsay, now the vicar of this parish. He had been a doctor in the Navy and had treated injured and ill slaves. She knew that he had only told a small portion of the horrors he had witnessed. And there was Madam Bouverie, such a gentle lady who owned the house and ran a hostel where beggars could be fed and clothed. Another glance took in quiet Lady Margaret Middleton herself, so gentle but strong, who seemed to steer many people towards living for God.

'Yes, this is an extraordinary place. There is so much kindness and grace here. Do you know? I hope it is catching! Then I could take it back with me to Cowslip Green, or Bath, or even London and share it round. Society outside seems so different. People have no thought for God's law or his love ...' William interrupted.

'You are right. Cards and drink ...'

'Or gossip and fashion ...'

'Not to mention the unfaithfulness and cruelty ...'

'This nation calls itself Christian, but it is nothing of the sort! We need a transformation of hearts and behaviour.'

'That is my desire too, Miss More. Only where do we begin?'

The conversations continued throughout their stay at Teston, and on through letters. So many ideas filled their heads. Wilberforce had plans for a new organisation. With the encouragement of so many friends, Hannah started to write. Men had written essays and arguments which would influence many, but a poem could strike directly at the emotions. It could be printed cheaply and would sell well because of Hannah's fame as a playwright. Hannah entitled it simply 'Slavery'.

'They have heads to think, and hearts to feel,
And souls to act,
For they have keen affections, kind desires,
Love strong as death ...' quoted Hannah to Mrs Garrick in her smart London drawing room.

'What do you think? I'm nearly finished, but just have to get this bit right. Oh, and listen to the next. I'm describing the snatching of slaves from their village.

"The burning village, and the blazing town:
See the dire victim torn from social life,
The shrieking babe, the agonizing wife!..."'
Mrs Garrick paused from her embroidery.

'Hannah, it is powerful, but do you not think it too upsetting? That bit about babies, for example; ladies might be too shocked, perhaps they'll think you are exaggerating? In fact, I am shocked!'

'But my aim is to shock, Eva! I have to get people to imagine, to put themselves in the place of the slaves before they will change their minds! If only we could all see that we're no different from those poor, poor slaves then everything would change very quickly indeed.'

Eva Garrick put down the embroidery onto a gilded table and her gracious smile hardened.

'I just don't know what to say, Hannah, my dear. I don't know if this is right – what would my dear

Mr Garrick have said? Is it right for a lady to be involved in politics like this? You no longer want to sit quietly with me. This new religion of yours has made you too active and changed your character. Fighting like this will just make you ill!'

The criticism from old friends hurt Hannah, but couldn't dissuade her from what she was doing. All the excitement of painted scenery and high drama in the theatre had made way for the tragedies of real life. She knew that Cowslip Green was not for escape but a centre of action. It was there that William came one evening after a day as a tourist in the nearby hills. He sat down to the dinner Hannah's maid had just placed on the snowy white cloth and cleared his throat.

'I have a proposal for you, Hannah.'

Hannah blinked with astonishment. William went on.

'I have a proposal concerning the villages in these valleys. I have returned to you today with empty pockets and a very sad heart. Have you ever travelled to Cheddar Gorge?' Hannah's momentary confusion disappeared. Of course, he wasn't proposing marriage! She blushed that she had even thought that for a moment.

'Yes, the beauty spot? Oh once, I think. The cliffs are magnificent aren't they, especially in summer when the trees clinging to the crags are in full leaf.' William interrupted, he seemed quite flustered.

'I'm not concerned with the scenery, Hannah, but with the people. I don't think I've seen poverty like it! The children crowded round the carriage and demanded money. Most were half clothed and filthy dirty. Their homes are in caves cut into the cliffs. We talked about wanting to bring change to people's lives; now here is something you can do!'

'Me?'

'You and Patty could bring great hope to these people. They haven't heard about God's love and they need to. You are teachers, you can teach them!'

Back to School

Hannah knocked at the door. She was standing in an extremely muddy farmyard having walked past a wild-looking dog, three pecking chickens and a gaggle of boys on their way to scare crows. She and Patty squeezed each other's hands as they waited for an answer. In this rough place, what kind of a reception would they receive?

'Oh! Ladies! Well, I'll just go and fetch my mistress.' They were left standing there and the heavy door closed in their faces.

'They certainly could do with some education in manners!' whispered Patty, but before she could go any further the door opened again and this time an older lady opened it. She smoothed her apron and looked the sisters in the eye.

'You're the ladies the vicar wrote about, I think? Come in then, you'll have to take us as you find us. My husband's just sat down; he's finished his dinner and doesn't like being disturbed.' She led them through a dimly lit hall to a parlour where there was a roaring fire and a large man slumped on a settle, an empty flagon next to him.

'James, it's those school teacher ladies to see you.' She poked her husband and then turned to Hannah and

Patty. 'Now, I don't suppose you'll be staying long. But you'll be wanting a drink?' She didn't wait for a reply but headed off down the passage as her husband roused himself and began to talk.

'The vicar said something about a school for the village. I'm surprised at that. What would the children in this village be wanting to read for?' Patty and Hannah hadn't expected this visit to be easy, but the farmer's disinterest was a surprise to them. As the wealthiest man in the village, Hannah had thought he would have some concern for his workers and their families. He continued, not registering the glances they exchanged.

'Now, I'm a man of business. I need to write and to do my sums for the farm and my children do too, for they'll take over when I'm gone and will need to manage things. But the workers and those weavers. Teach them to read and they'll just give me trouble. You can be sure of that.' He folded his arms as if that was the end of the matter. Patty seemed to shrink, but though Hannah was surprised, she wasn't daunted. The farmer's wife came in at that point with a jug of cider. She filled up her husband's flagon and poured a generous helping into mugs for Hannah and Patty.

'Oh cider, how refreshing! I saw your orchard as the carriage drove up the lane. You have some fine trees there. I grow some fruit myself, just berries mainly, and I have real trouble with the birds. Can't keep them away! I suppose you don't have that trouble here?' The farmer's wife, who had lingered suspiciously, brightened up.

'Not with birds. Our trouble is with the boys. As soon as the crop is ripe, they come up from the village in gangs and scrump the ripest apples. Not just the fallen ones too, but the ones at the top of the tree! They're in and out in a flash and I can hardly do a thing about it. My James here, if he caught them, he'd give them a thrashing, now wouldn't you?' Her husband joined in.

'That I would! Cheeky vermin. How dare they! You see, Miss More, they're bad enough already. If you were to teach these ragamuffins a lesson they'd just get cleverer at cheating me. They need work, hard work. That teaches them respect and to know their place. Look out of that window, see that boy?'

'One of the ones we met in the yard? Yes I see him.' replied Patty as she watched the raggle-taggle boy standing in the centre of the field waving his arms slowly up and down. He looked cold and bored, she thought.

'They're my bird-scarers. Keep the birds off the new-sown seed. Now that tires them out and keeps them out of mischief. They work dawn till dusk for a few pennies they can give to their mothers. Now that is proper charity if you ask me. I give them the work and they do the work. You town people with your fancy clothes and fancy talk just don't understand.' The farmer smiled smugly, quite pleased with his rudeness, but Hannah wouldn't give up.

'This is really excellent cider, Mr Nailer, thank you. I do in part agree with you. Boys can be so naughty, not knowing right from wrong, and they can be lazy too, can't they? You might tell me that I'm a fussy spinster schoolteacher who doesn't understand business, but I do see your problems. Listen to me just for a moment before you close your mind. Now, you keep those boys busy six days a week, don't you?'

'Yes, six days. We're respectable folk, you know, always keep the Lord's Day and give the villagers a rest then. They don't really deserve it though, give them time off and they're in trouble fast as can be. Those people need a strong hand I can tell you.' The farmer looked quite affronted so Hannah hurried on, smiling warmly as she spoke.

'So Sundays are when they steal the apples, or go roaring up and down the lanes? Maybe that's when their fathers go and drink their money away in the inns and when the cock fights happen. What a load of trouble you have, managing these folk! But imagine that we had care of those same boys on a Sunday afternoon. We could keep them out of mischief, and teach them how to behave. We'd be teaching your people God's Word, Mr Nailer, which tells us all to obey those in charge, to work hard and earn our bread honestly. Don't you think your bird-scarers would do a better job for you if you let us teach them the Scriptures?'

The farmer rubbed his bristly chin, thinking a while, but his wife spoke up.

'It seems to me that you're talking sense. This might be a saving of money, not a waste. Let me get you some seed cake, while you talk more.' She strode out of the room, and as she did, in tumbled two little girls with a puppy. They were dressed plainly and curls escaped from their matching red ribbons. As they caught sight of Hannah and Patty, they ran to hide behind their fathers' chair. Hannah laughed and took a piece of gingerbread out of her pocket.

'I can see you have your hands full at home as well as outside. Come here girls, I have something for you …' And for the rest of the afternoon, Hannah and Patty were occupied, planning a school as well as playing with the farmer's children.

Some months later, Patty and Hannah arrived again at the village. They'd been many times in the intervening months, persuading, negotiating and inspecting, but this was a special day. After a short service they walked down the lane from the church to a large, freshly whitewashed barn accompanied by a great crowd of children. Some of their parents were there too and so were the farmer and his family. The vicar, who only visited his parish occasionally, had come for the special day. Most of the children were barefoot and all looked thin and ragged, but they cheered and joked as they ran ahead, trying to catch a glimpse of these two grand ladies, their teachers. Into the barn they processed and the children took their places on narrow benches whilst the adults stood around the edge. Hannah stood in front of them all, beaming and raised her voice.

'Welcome everyone to the opening of the Cheddar Sunday School. Shall we pray before we begin?'

That evening, the More sisters sat down in the village inn with Sarah, the teacher they'd employed to help them. She was to live in the village and visit families during the week as well as set up other classes in the evenings, whilst Patty and Hannah would visit most Sundays to teach the children.

'Before we leave tomorrow morning, I must remind you of your duties, Sarah,' began Hannah. 'You are here in this village as a light, to share God's love with the children and their families. Remember they know so little of him. Patty, when we were going through the village cottages, how many Bibles did we find? Was it one or two?'

'One I think, and that was being used as a flower-pot stand! Under a very pretty red geranium, as I recall!'

'You're right, one Bible in a village of two hundred houses. It is no wonder that the people of Cheddar spend their money on drink and have no care how they live. Sarah, always remember why we are starting this school. Children need to read so that they can read the Word of God. Once they can do that, then our Lord can, and we pray, will, transform this village. Of course, we want to help the very poor live better lives, but that will only happen when they can hear God's voice.'

Sarah stared down at her feet resting on the stone flags of the floor. She seemed to be thinking hard.

'Miss More, you know that with all my heart I agree with you. But when I see how wretched the homes are here and how rude and surly the parents are, I do feel at a loss. How am I to manage?'

Hannah nodded. 'The girls I have taught were smart and polite, a far cry from these wild village children. But isn't our method the same? Sarah, you love the Lord Jesus, so show that love to them. Keep lessons short, sing songs, give rewards; gingerbread will win many hearts! We must demonstrate that to be religious is to be loving, not dour or harsh. Patty and I will be here all the weeks we can, to help you in your teaching.'

And so they were. Patty and Hannah together found themselves busier than ever. Their carriage took them down the narrow, often muddy lanes week by week, and slowly they became known and liked by farmers and workers alike. But between those Sundays, the sisters were busy too. Once they had started in one village they found out about other, sometimes needier, places. The Mendips were an area with beautiful rolling hills and rustic looking farms, but they also contained factories and mines where workers faced danger every day. Hannah and Patty found themselves talking to dirty working people in glass factories, next to the furnaces which belched out soot and flames, and in homes which had mine shafts within them. Though they had grown up in a poor family, squeezed into a tiny home, they had been taught well and wisely. These families had no-one to teach them or care for them. After two years were up, the sisters were running schools in seven villages. Out of the schools had sprung societies to help women save money, evening classes for adults and teenagers, annual feasts and parties. The sisters were known and respected by many, though there were a few who wanted to cause problems.

As the schools grew and behaviour changed in the villages, the vicars of some of the villages took note. Men and women were turning to Christ and spending time together reading the Bible and praying. This all looked a little suspicious. Surely the village church was the place for religion, not homes or schools? What if these new believers got ideas above their station and turned against their employers? Now they could read the Bible, they could also read political books as well. Education was a dangerous thing!

Runaways and Revolutions

Whilst Hannah was hard at work setting up schools in the hidden valleys of Somerset, there was revolution across the English Channel in France. In 1789, the year Cheddar school was opened, the Bastille prison was stormed by crowds of rioters. They were hungry and angry, sick of the cruel disinterest of the royal family which had left them in poverty. In ragged clothes they marched through the streets of Paris singing and shouting. They demanded freedom, brotherhood and equality. Hannah and her friends were thrilled at this exciting news. The unfair political system was bound to change, and the very poorest of French society would be cared for. Her joy didn't last long though, as reports from France started to tell of murder, destruction of religion and the dreaded guillotine. Catholic priests became refugees and Hannah's sisters provided a temporary shelter for some of them in their new house in Bath.

But at the same time as one crisis was erupting in France, another small crisis came very near to Hannah's home. A letter arrived at the house Hannah's sisters shared in Bath.

'You must come straight away. Clementina has run away.'

So they did. Packing a few belongings, the five More sisters rushed to their old school in Bristol. Not long ago they had handed it over to a dear young friend, Selina Mills, and now she was desperate for help. Rushing them into her study, Selina closed the door behind her and began to weep. There was no fire in the grate and a mess of papers lay on the desk. Selina looked as though she'd been awake all night.

'Poor, poor girl, it wasn't your fault!' soothed Sally as she embraced Selina. 'We're here now. You must tell us exactly what has happened and we'll see what we can do.' Patty hurried quietly out of the room to find things to light the fire and Hannah sat down ready to listen.

Selina took a deep breath. 'Clementina.' She took another breath. 'Clementina, well you know what she is like, you're her guardians. She's fourteen and romantic. Just a young girl, easily carried away, and with all that money held in trust for her. Once she comes of age she'll have a fortune and that is the problem! I think she was happy here; she seemed to be at any rate. But there was a doctor, well actually more of a chemist, he's called Richard Perry. And he watched the girls. I think he was watching for her, waiting for when we took the girls out for a walk, and he sent her letters, love letters.'

'Love letters?'

'Yes, secret letters claiming that he was in love with her. Though, of course, we didn't find this out till it was too late. And then yesterday she asked permission to go and visit her aunt. It seemed innocent enough so I let her go.'

'And now she's run away with him?'

'Yes, to Gretna Green to get married. It is like one of those dreadful novels. But this is real. If they get there and marry, all her money will be his.'

'And that is the only thing he wants!' interrupted Hannah grimly. 'Poor, silly girl. All it took was a couple of swooning letters and she threw away this safe home for a dream of romance! Now, you said in your letter that your brother has followed them in a carriage?'

'Yes, my brother and sister have. They left as soon as we worked out what had happened. If the driver can only catch them up and stop the coach before they are married, then maybe she can be saved.'

It was a few days drive on a rough road to Gretna Green, the village just over the border into Scotland where couples could marry quickly. It was a rough road, but one well-travelled by eloping couples in the eighteenth century. To Clementina it seemed a fantastic adventure and to Richard Perry it was the perfect way to get very rich, very quickly.

Clementina began to scream again and again as blood crept down her face. Richard too was bleeding and the sight of his handsome face, sticky with blood, caused her to scream even more. Their coach had been driving so fast that it had overturned, damaging passengers, driver and horses alike. Sadly, this wasn't enough to delay the marriage; patched up with bandages they found another ride and raced over the border. They made their vows in a very short ceremony. No friends or family were there, just a couple of old men pulled out of the pub as witnesses. Clementina and Richard didn't seem to mind though. They had each other and now no one could separate them. Clementina beamed as she clung on to Richard's arm and gazed up at him. The cuts on her face didn't matter now. She had a husband! How grown up she felt! How all the other girls at school would be jealous! She was a Mrs and could live in style with her darling Richard. Richard was smiling too, and was feeling smug as well. He was now a wealthy man; his pretty, silly wife had opened the door to all kind of pleasures. It was on the way back that Selina's brother and sister met the newly-weds, two carriages squeezing past each other on the northern road. They were too late.

Hannah was with Selina when she heard this news. She was in despair. Would parents remove their daughters from the school, when they heard of the scandal? What would Clementina do? She'd been brought up in a sheltered, wealthy home and now she was married to a money-grabbing chemist, who surely would lose interest in her once he had her money. But the law was all in his favour. Once married, women lost all their right to own property. Hannah rushed to London nevertheless and raced around the capital seeking advice from friends.

'Bishop Porteus, I am so grateful that you would see me. You've heard of ...'

'Of course, how could I not. You are in the papers again Hannah, and it isn't favourable!'

'I'm not surprised. A man snatches away a young impressionable girl and he is made a hero by the press. All I can think of is Clementina. I want to find out where she is, and then I want to see if we can take this Perry man to court.' The Bishop sighed. Hannah's determination was impressive, but he doubted whether even Hannah would solve this problem.

'My dear, I think you need a lawyer, not a Bishop! Someone who knows the ins and outs of the law. The problem is, you and I know that Perry has done something dreadful, but will a judge think that? If Clementina went with him willingly then there is really nothing to be done.'

Hannah didn't give up. She wanted to help not only Clementina but also Selina; if the school failed because of this publicity, then she would lose her home and income too. Traipsing round London Hannah eventually found the lodging place of the couple, but when she got there she found that Perry had a gun. It was time to retreat.

'Guns, kidnap, heiresses! I felt for a month that I was a character in a novel!' Hannah later reflected as she sat in a carriage with Patty making their way through Bath. 'We all were. And it didn't have a happy ending. I had to give up fighting for Clementina; but I feel that I mustn't give up fighting for other girls like her.'

'How do you mean?' asked Patty, intrigued.

'You know I've just written a book about how the wealthy need to take God seriously, to try to wake up some of those respectable folk ...'

'Yes, Hannah. Are you going to tell me that you're going to write another one? Do you have time? We've got the schools to think about and you said that there are more villages which ...'

Hannah interrupted her sister, whose face seemed to be growing redder by the minute.

'Patty, I am. Now, you must trust God. He has given me only so many years on Earth and I intend to use them well. The schools are for the poor, I care for them deeply, but I care for the rich too, and for girls especially. Look around you.'

It was time for the dancing to start. Other carriages flew down the wide streets of Bath with their colourful coachmen driving the horses hard. Patty and Hannah watched as a group of ladies were being handed down from a red carriage outside the assembly rooms. The light from torches danced off the long feathers in their hair and their brightly coloured cloaks. The ladies giggled together and their laughter rang down the wet streets. Hannah went on.

'Maybe I'm getting old! The young people now seem so frivolous; under their cloaks they are like Eve, wearing next to nothing and shameless too! Oh, I do sound old don't I?'

Patty nodded but it didn't stop Hannah.

'Girls are being brought up to think that the only important things in life are balls and dresses and finding a husband. They don't fear God or care about others.'

'Hannah!' chided Patty, 'you do sound cross. Maybe we weren't like that because we didn't have the chance. We were poor and had to earn money. We didn't have time for balls and parties!' She looked out of the carriage again. 'But you are right. It has always been the case? Rich or poor, we all run after what is bright and empty unless God wins our hearts.'

The carriage rumbled on and the sisters fell silent. Bath wasn't like Teston or Cowslip Green, places of rest and escape; instead it was a bit like being back in London, a playground for the rich. Invalids came to take the waters in the hope of being cured, but most people came to flirt or watch others flirt. There were balls every night and plenty of places to gamble or get drunk.

Hannah watched a group of young men in uniform swagger along the street, already half drunk. She wasn't going to be put off her new idea.

'I want to write a book which will help mothers and teachers. They are the ones who can give girls some ambition. Clementina had her head turned and threw away her so many opportunities; I hear that she's excited now about her baby, but soon she'll find out how hard it is to be on your own. We can't change that now, but maybe I can help other families. Girls shouldn't be thinking that they are just made for pleasure and decoration. I can show them how important they are and what good they can do in this world! Perhaps I can show their mothers how to teach them about the Lord.'

Yet whilst Hannah's heart was being stirred to write about the good women could do, her friends were keen to see her writing something else. News from France had become much more worrying as the revolution progressed. Instead of a new age of justice, there was terror on the streets.

> *There was no resistance; the unhappy victims were butchered like sheep at a slaughter house ....They were handed out of the prison door two by two into the Rue Vaugerard, where their throats were cut.*

Bishop Porteus put down his newspaper. He turned in his chair to Hannah.

'Those are priests who are being murdered by the mob. If I was there in France, I would be torn limb from limb. I can't believe that it has come to this; confusion and slaughter so near to home. I fear for us here in Britain.'

They were sitting in the Bishop's warm study in London. A good breakfast had been eaten and Hannah was soon going to be on her way to her publishers' office. Surely, nowhere could be safer? But the Bishop was right. The people in France had overthrown the Government and King and Church, and there were plenty in England who were keen to do the same.

'And I fear too, Bishop. When I visit my schools and go into the cottages and sit and talk with the villagers I often hear anger. Sometimes the farmers don't pay them enough and they go without food. They are proud people. Revolution is a tempting thought to them. And there are plenty of others who are only too happy to stir up trouble.' Hannah looked up glumly at the rows of orderly books. England was a much fairer place than France, it was true, but there was still real suffering and hardship. Revolution wouldn't get rid of that though. It would only bring greater problems. Bishop Porteus watched her and smiled.

'You are the one person I know who really understands the poor. You must use your talents for such a time as this!'

Hannah left soon after for her publisher, mulling those thoughts over in her mind. She imagined the streets she drove down full of blood thirsty crowds, the preachers silenced and leaders persecuted. Maybe it was time to write not for the rich again, but for the poor. So, very quickly, that afternoon, she dashed off a short story about friends arguing in a pub. She wrote quite differently from how she'd written before. There were no long words or flowery phrases. Instead she wrote as the everyday people spoke, and spiced it with plenty of humour. In the story she showed that rebellion was pointless and that only by trusting in God and working hard could anyone be happy.

More Stories

The story was a success. Hannah received a letter telling her how the royal family had enjoyed it, which wasn't really her plan; she'd meant it for poor working men!

As the months passed, it became clear that England would not follow France into a bloody revolution. Instead England was at war with France. But with war and some bad harvests came food shortages. The poor, as always, were the ones who suffered the most.

'Miss More, Miss More, can I have a moment please?'

Hannah was showing her friend around a nearby workhouse, where the unemployed were sent to work in exchange for terrible food and basic shelter. Hannah was already feeling overwhelmed by the poverty she saw around her, so she wasn't prepared for the news she was about to hear.

'My name is James Overstock. I've come from Blagdon.'

'Blagdon, near Cowslip Green? Yes, go on.' Hannah was surprised to be stopped by this smartly dressed man. He looked like a farmer in his Sunday best.

'I'm the church warden, and I've come to ask for your help. You see, we're having dreadful trouble.'

Hannah looked at his anxious face and invited him to sit down on the dirty bench.

'There's a woman who stole some butter.' Hannah looked confused. Butter was hardly a problem.

'She couldn't afford any, the price it was, and neither could any of her neighbours. This woman, she got a group of them together, mothers and grandmothers and children. They marched into the shop, shouting and ranting. You've never seen the like, not in Somerset, at any rate. We thought there was going to be a riot! And then she went and stole the butter she needed. So now she's been sentenced to death. The whole village is in uproar. The neighbours won't be satisfied, but the farmers and the vicar are terrified. No one will work … We thought maybe you and your sister could help. Everyone else is too scared to come.' Mr Overstock paused and looked hopefully to Hannah. She sighed.

'You think two spinsters can sort this out? I don't know what to say!' Hannah shook her head. Her reputation had clearly spread, but quite what she and Patty could do in this dangerous place she didn't know.

'Come and talk to the people. Calm them down and get them settled. Then maybe you could start a school. It might bring some order. Help the children and the mothers.' He smiled at her and Hannah slowly nodded her head.

'We'll come,' she said.

So that was another school. Hannah and Patty worked hard to establish it and find the right teacher. It wasn't an easy task, especially when they had so many other schools and clubs to look after. The schools cost money as well, and so did the club, and the secret gifts Hannah gave to individuals. Hannah encouraged her wealthy friends to give generously and, as usual, she dipped between the two worlds. One week she might be in a cottage attending to an ill grandmother, the next she could find herself dressed up and talking to a titled lady. Whoever she was with though, she knew that they had the same need: to turn to Christ and to follow him.

With such a relentless life, Hannah often suffered from migraines. On Monday mornings, after teaching in several village schools on the Sunday, she often found herself in bed and unable to move. Winter was a time for recuperation though; Cowslip Green was delightful in the summer but draughty and damp in the winter and the lanes to the villages were mired in mud, so Patty and she retired to their sisters' home in Bath. There she could sit and talk a while.

'We do forget how the poor have the same tastes, appetites and feelings that we have. They haven't had the benefit of education, but they can enjoy a good story, just as we do.' Hannah was in the warm drawing room of the tall Bath townhouse. Elizabeth Bouverie had come from Teston to visit and they, as usual, were talking about books.

Her friend Elizabeth nodded. 'That is true; downstairs I often hear one servant girl reading out a story from a cheap pamphlet to the rest. They love to hear a romance or a ghost story. They shriek out loud or giggle, just as girls in your sisters' school would, Hannah.'

'Oh, I remember those books! Sold in the market for a few pennies and then passed around – I did enjoy the fairy tales. My absolute favourite was Cinderella I think. I loved the ugly sisters and the ending, of course ... then there was Tom Thumb and Jack and the Beanstalk. But, Elizabeth, often the books aren't fairy tales.' Hannah's face became sombre. 'There are plenty of ghost stories and murders, or tales of girls running away with their lovers. Most of those make sin seem exciting and goodness seem so dull. How wretched! We teach children to read. But what they read tells them lies. Remember Clementina? Maybe she wouldn't have run away if she'd not read some of those romances.'

Elizabeth saw how upset Patty looked and poured another cup of tea.

'Maybe so, maybe not. Let's not dwell on Clementina, we can trust God to look after her, wherever she is now. Let me tell you some news. I saw Wilberforce last week and we had a long talk about the campaign. He tells me that whilst we are at war with France there will be no change in the laws about slavery; the Prime Minister is too busy trying to defeat the French to think about the poor slaves. I just wonder when the Lord will act ... Still we must continue to do all we can ... I hear that the boycott of sugar is still going on, and there are always letters to write. Tell me, Patty, how is the new school in Blagdon?'

Patty was relieved to talk about the great progress in the village. Whole families were involved in learning from the Bible and many were going along to church as well. Hannah, meanwhile, seemed to have drifted off into a daydream as she rested her chin on her hand and looked out through the window onto the elegant street of four-storeyed houses. Their white stucco fronts all looked the same and there was not a tree in sight. Hannah missed her home, but was thinking more about the villagers, huddled in their cottages or out at work in the cold mist. They couldn't escape the hardships of winter as she could. The school's work was far beyond what she'd dreamed, but still it was so little and the need was so great. Mention of William Wilberforce had reminded her of his other great passion; to change the culture of Britain for the good.

All of a sudden she interrupted the conversation.

'What I think we need to be doing is writing our own stories and songs, ones which will do good, not harm. And we can arrange for them to be sold, just as these awful ones are, in the markets and the lanes. Our schools are only in a few villages, but we could reach the whole country this way. Imagine them now, sitting round their little fires, the women knitting, the children all with a job to do, or when they are out in the fields working in a team. Imagine if they could tell each other good stories or rhymes. I know some have

God's Word – and we give out Bibles in our clubs – but imagine if they were to have stories which put Bible truths into lives like theirs!'

Elizabeth and Patty laughed nervously, not what Hannah was expecting.

'You are so naughty!' Elizabeth scolded. 'You weren't listening to us at all, were you? You spent all that time plotting!' But after the teasing the two women sat and listened. Hannah did have lots of ideas and her urgency was contagious.

'I shall ask all my friends to invest in the scheme. We need money to get the works printed and then more money to send them around the country. They will be sold, but at a reduced price, so the very poorest will want to buy them. What do you think?'

Patty took a deep breath. 'Hannah, you've so often tired yourself out with your schemes. You'll just end up in bed, ill again. No, listen to me.' She ignored Hannah who was about to object.

'I'm not wanting to stop you. It is a brilliant idea. But perhaps you need help with the writing as well as the money? I'm sure the bishop can write a story, and we can too, can't we? Well, maybe not me, I'm best at teaching, but I'm sure Sally can lend a hand. We can all take part Hannah, and then more good will be done.'

And so it was. The 'Cheap Repository Tracts' got off the ground. Hannah sat at her desk, quill in hand, writing rapidly. It wasn't difficult for her as she was writing about what she saw everyday.

Betty Brown, the Orange Girl, was born nobody knows where, and bred nobody knows how. The longest thing that Betty can remember is that she used to crawl up out of a night cellar, stroll about the streets and pick cinders from the scavengers' carts.' Hannah paused. She'd had this story buzzing about her head for a week and she could just imagine Betty in her mind's eye. This Betty was quick and ambitious, though she was very poor. She borrowed money from the dreadful Mrs Sponge so that she could buy a barrow to sell oranges in the street. What Betty didn't realise, however, was that the money she paid Mrs Sponge every day for food and lodging and interest was far more than she had borrowed in the first place. Hannah carried on.

She crept up to bed in one of Mrs Sponge's garrets, five storeys high. This loft, to be sure, had no window, but what it wanted in light was made up in company, as it had three beds, and thrice as many lodgers.'

Now, how to help poor Betty? Hannah knew only one way. There was to be a kind lady who would give help and advice as well as tell her about Jesus, and then Betty, though going through a few more trials, would have some success.

She rose in the world till at length she came to keep that handsome sausage shop near the Seven Dials, and was married to an honest coachman.'

There, the story was done. She leant back in her chair and rubbed her aching head. Was another migraine coming or did she just need some air? When this was done there was her book on women's education to get back to, then there were school accounts to look over. It was going to be a late night.

The next morning, a letter arrived which meant that Hannah didn't get back to her book that day or the next. It was from the vicar's sister at Blagdon and was the beginning of the worst period in her life.

'I am in despair,' she told William Wilberforce. The vicar, Thomas Bere, was teaching his congregation that they didn't need to pay any attention to the Bible and that Jesus is not God's Son, but then he complained that Hannah had brought in a school teacher who did teach people the Bible.

'He says that I must get rid of my school teacher, he says he's an extremist who is causing trouble. But I think I would rather close the school than give in to such a bully. Children have stopped coming to school because of his threats. All I want is for the Bible to be taught. How am I to achieve that when Mr Bere only wants to fight?' Wilberforce, as always, gave good advice.

'You must go to the bishop and ask him to sort it out. You concentrate on what you need to do, Hannah. Don't give up.' So Hannah began writing more letters. Eventually, after writing lots of letters, it became clear to everyone that the vicar was in the wrong.

That result, though, lead to more problems. Bere lost his job and, full of rage, published a book all about the arguments. Suddenly, the fight was no longer about a village school, but about the freedom to believe the Bible. Hannah and many of her friends were turned upon in the newspapers and cruel pamphlets. It was said that they were against the church and full of wild, revolutionary ideas. Again and again, Hannah was attacked as an unnatural woman who was greedy for power. She remained silent. Replying to her accusers would only make the problem worse, but it was really hard to see her reputation ruined and all her hard work misunderstood.

'It goes against the grain to say nothing, Patty.' Hannah said one evening before bed. 'So, we won't buy another newspaper; it is too painful to read what they are saying about me.'

'I think you're right. This will pass though; they'll lose interest in the end. And we still have the school. That is the most important thing.' Hannah took a sip of her drink and sighed. For so much of her young life she'd longed to be important and famous and she'd achieved that. Now she was learning what it was to give that up.

'I take great comfort from remembering how Jesus was scorned and was accused. He was silent. That is what helps me not to retaliate. My fame was too dear to me. So this trial is a blessing, Patty, the Lord has taken my reputation away so that I might love Him more. Now, let's go up to bed.'

'You know, Patty, I think I can get back to work on my book.' Hannah said one day a year later. She had been ill for a long time, but now her strength was returning. The spring sunlight was streaming in through the bedroom window of her new house. Cowslip Green had been lovely, but was too small and too damp. In the midst of the Blagdon troubles, Hannah had started to build a new house only half a mile away, and now she was there. It was called Barley Wood and was big enough to hold plenty of visitors.

'First, though, I am going to walk through the gardens.' Hannah took up her stick and put on her hat and went out to inspect her flower beds. There was much work to be done, Hannah was pleased to observe. Gardening was such a perfect rest from writing, and these lawns would be a wonderful place for children to play. She would invite the Wilberforce children down, and Selina's son. There was a place to grow strawberries and by the wall a peach tree could perhaps be trained. Hannah smiled. Barley Wood was going to be a delightful home.

The Final Chapter

Hannah was in bed. Around her were neat piles of books, a small writing box for letters and flowers from her garden. This was where she spent most of her time these days, interrupted by many visitors, reading, writing and knitting.

Right now she was reading a letter.

'It grieves me to let you know that a mutual friend has written to me to say that your servants are not behaving as you would expect.'

She put the letter down and was still for a moment. Maybe she had feared this, but it was still a shock.

'I have heard that some nights they will all take off to the village for parties, leaving you completely on your own. The manager of your land is taking much of the profit for himself and all of them are wasting money and food. I urge you to take urgent action.'

What was she to do? For twenty-four years she had lived at Barley Wood, and, after Patty had died nine years ago, she had completely relied upon her eight servants for everything. She could barely leave her bedroom. Instead, they tended her garden, managed her farmland, repaired the house and cooked and served her food, and looked after her frequent guests; indeed, they felt more like family than paid workers.

Hannah looked at the pretty display of roses that Louisa had brought in a few hours ago. The fragrance was still in the air of the bedroom. I suppose I must bear some of the blame, Hannah reflected sadly. There isn't really the work for them all. I've been trying to be generous and keep them all, I haven't wanted to let them go. So they've grown bored and lazy. And I'm stuck up here. No wonder the servants think how they behave doesn't matter.

Hannah laid the letter on her quilt and looked out of the window. Maybe her days at Barley Wood were over. It would be hard to leave. Hannah had such special memories of the place. There were the times when she, Patty and Betty had sat on the lawn surrounded by the children of her friends. She'd told them stories and they'd eaten strawberries, fresh from the garden, together. Now those children were famous adults themselves. There had been visits from so many interesting people; poets and writers, politicians and ministers. She'd met missionaries and teachers here and had debated and written and gardened and cooked. What blessings God had brought her at Barley Wood!

In the corner of the room, her pet squirrel woke up and scurried towards the bed. The songbirds in a cage startled by the noise, began to sing. Hannah reached for the bell and rang for Louisa.

'My dear, there are some questions I need to ask you.' She began. 'I know you think that I'm a bit like one of those birds!' Hannah paused to watch Louisa's face. She looked confused.

'Yes you do! You think that I'm trapped up here, a rather spoilt old lady who doesn't know anything about real life, left alone in a rather pretty cage whilst all the wild birds sing and fly outside.'

Louisa smiled nervously. Miss More was usually polite and cheerful, what was she talking about? Was she ill?

'And you and the groom and the gardener and the cook are those wild birds who don't really care for the spoilt caged birds because you can enjoy your freedom.' She watched Louisa again whose smile started to droop.

'I see you understand me! Louisa, my dear, I don't wish to play games with you, but you must know that this old bird,' she lifted her lace-gloved hand and pointed at herself, 'knows what is going on downstairs.' Louisa looked down at her neat boots and then out of the window. She couldn't look her benefactor in the eye.

'Miss More. If you're talking about the parties, it was only once or twice, and it was Jack who suggested them, it was never my idea. I didn't really want to do it …' She trailed off because she had looked at Hannah's face. Hannah was teasing no longer and she looked old and sad.

'I said, Louisa, that I don't wish to play games. I know some of what you and the others have done. There

107

has been laziness and theft at the very least. You and I both know that it is wrong. I have taught you myself and arranged work for you when your parents couldn't care for you. And for as long as you've been under my roof, you have been taught that we are all sinners who need God's forgiveness. You and the others need to go to him, first of all, and leave your excuses behind. I will not be punishing you, but I think we all will have to leave Barley Wood.'

When Louisa finally left the pretty bedroom that afternoon, after tears and prayers and hugs, Hannah felt quite exhausted. The shock of discovering that those she had treated as family had betrayed her, was sinking in. It definitely was the right time to leave, so now she must write to friends and ask their advice about buying and selling houses, about new places for the servants and about furniture and gardens. It was at times like these, that she missed Patty and her other sisters painfully. They would all have known what to do.

It was only a few weeks later, that Hannah stood in her garden looking up at the house to say goodbye. Around her, daffodils were starting to open and through the house windows she could see dust sheets being put on the furniture. She had already said goodbye to the servants. New jobs had been found for them and Hannah was convinced they had learned their lesson. She would be leaving herself later in the day to a new home in the very area of Bristol where the school had been. She hadn't wanted to go back to that noisy city, but it couldn't be helped.

'I shall count my blessings,' she said to a robin which was looking at her quizzically.

'That has always helped. Though I'm sure I won't be able to count them all. First, the Lord of all creation has shown me mercy! He has rescued me from my sin and bought me a great inheritance. Then, number two, he's given me such friends to help me along towards heaven and, third, he's has given me work to do. Since I first trusted in his grace I've not been bored for one moment. And, what number am I at now? Yes, four, I think, he's kept changing me too. Some days I've been so cross with myself and my sin, but then He's helped me by his Holy Spirit.' Hannah smiled as she looked around the garden. 'I love this place, especially the garden, sometimes I've thought more about these plants than their creator! In town I won't be able to do that. I shall prepare my mind for heaven.' She called to her companion for an arm to lean on and together they made their way to the waiting carriage.

Hannah spent the next five and a half years in a neat town house. Her doctors were close at hand to visit her in her illnesses, which seemed to follow one after another. Other visitors came too, those who had heard of her schools and read her books. They wanted to hear the famous lady's wit and opinions, but so many were they that visiting hours had to be limited to allow

Hannah to rest, for that was really all Hannah wanted now, the rest of heaven.

'If only I could know that all the slaves had been set free, then I would be ready to die in peace!' she wrote in a letter to a friend. But it wasn't so. The trading of slaves had been banned almost twenty years before, but farmers could still own a slave in many of Britain's colonies, and so, as slaves had children the new generation was enslaved. Slavery went on and on, trapping many in its cruel web. How could it be stopped but by a change in the law? Her dearest friend William Wilberforce had retired from Parliament and so younger men were continuing to fight for real freedom for the oppressed slaves. But Wilberforce, Hannah and many others prayed daily for this change. There was other work she prayed for from her bed too. One visitor remarked upon her bookshelf.

'Yes, take a close look,' said Hannah gesturing at the fine leather bound volumes. 'They are all mine! I think of the girl I was, hiding under the stairs and scribbling. I had no idea that my stories and poems would be read across the world. Do you know that I am all the rage in America, and my last book on prayer is being translated into Dutch?' She grinned. 'I can hardly believe it myself, and I can't really believe that my words have done much good whatever language they're in. Do you know what I think the best thing my books have done?'

Her smart clergyman visitor shook his head. Miss Hannah More had a reputation for eccentricity, and she certainly seemed to be talking strangely now. She seemed rather over-excited.

'It is the money!' She paused, squinting at him to see how he was responding. He certainly looked embarrassed; talking about wealth was really not good manners. And a Christian lady pleased to be rich! He didn't know where to look.

'Oh, come now, I'm teasing you! I didn't want the money for myself, but for the good it could do for others. My books may have helped some people as they have read, but the money I've earned from them has enabled me to help many more! They have paid for the schools where many families have met Christ and been set free from poverty. They have paid for many Bibles to be given away in, oh, I forget how many countries! And even now whilst my hands can do very little, my money can do great good and my prayers can do even more.'

'You are so right Miss More. You have done remarkable things.' He smiled, thinking he was on safe territory once more. But he wasn't!

'Fiddlesticks! Don't praise me; praise the Lord. I've only done very little, and what I've done was done with others. My sisters and Mr Wilberforce, the teachers in the schools and all my friends. The Lord has done remarkable things, we've just been his servants.'

Not long after this conversation, Hannah received a visit from a Doctor with a newspaper. Though unwell she'd been hoping for some news, and what the Doctor read out to her was the best she could possibly have heard. Parliament had passed the Bill for the abolition of the slave trade! The freedom she and so many of her friends had been praying for for more than forty years had come about. The slaves were free!

Three days later she heard sad news. William Wilberforce, his great life goal accomplished, had died in his sleep. Hannah herself was growing more tired and ill by the day. She was satisfied though, and a few months later Hannah followed her friend to glory.

Postscript

Hannah More lived through extraordinary years of change in Europe. When she was born men, women and children could be bought and sold like animals, cross-cultural missionary work was hardly thought of and the poor children stood no chance of education. By the end of her life slavery had been abolished in British territories and many ordinary people were leaving their homes to take the gospel overseas. Schools had been set up for adults and children in many poor areas and wealthy girls were taught not just to be decorative but to work hard and do good. Hannah More had a hand in all these changes. She worked with others to transform society for the better and her legacy lasted way beyond her years. Though Hannah didn't think her books were that important, they were read in many countries for years after her death, helping poor and rich alike to focus their hearts on Jesus. Schools were named after her in North America, England and Asia and some of them still exist today.

Thinking Further Topics

The First School

1. Hannah's mother wanted Hannah to continue with lessons, but her father didn't. Why do you think they felt like this?

2. Are you grateful for your education or do you sometimes moan? In eighteenth-century England poor children often didn't go to school, but rich boys did. Girls, whether rich or poor were often hardly educated at all. This is still the case in some countries today. Often Christian charities work to provide education for girls in places where the government can't, or won't run schools. Could you do anything to support a charity like this?

3. In the chapter Hannah remembers women from the Bible who were brave and strong like Abigail, Ruth and Lydia. Why don't you look up one of their stories in the Bible (1 Samuel 25, Ruth, Acts 16). What can you learn from them about how girls and women can use their talents today?

New Plans

1. Mary, Hannah's oldest sister, was only a teenager when she started her school. Isn't that amazing! Do you think people around you expect young people to do hard and brave things like that or not? Should they?

2. Hannah and her sisters didn't know much about slavery even though they lived a few miles away from Bristol, one of the main slave trading ports. How would you describe their attitude to slavery? Why do you think they weren't really angry about it? Sometimes we too can accept an activity which is very wrong because people all around us think it is okay. How should we decide whether something is acceptable or not?

Do not conform any longer to the pattern of this world, but be transformed by the renewing of your mind. Then you will be able to test and approve what God's will is – his good, pleasing and perfect will (Romans 12:2).

Drama!

1. What is it about the chattering schoolgirls that annoyed Hannah? In what ways is she like them? Are you like them at all?

2. The theatre is an exciting place to be. Hannah disapproved of many of the plays that were put on. Why do you think she felt like this?

3. Not so many people go to the theatre now, but they do watch films or TV. What are your favourites? Do

115

these shows help you to act well or do they make bad behaviour look cool or funny?

... Whatever is true, whatever is noble, whatever is right, whatever is pure, whatever is lovely, whatever is admirable — if anything is excellent or praiseworthy — think about such things (Philippians 4:8).

Love Story

1. Planning for the future is very exciting, but it caused problems for Hannah. Where was she putting her trust in this chapter?

2. The very wealthy in eighteenth-century England did not have to work for their money. They relied on income from land they owned or family money which had been invested. If Hannah had married William Turner, it would have meant the whole family would have been provided for. What else would Hannah have gained from the marriage? Can you see any difficulties which could have occurred if he'd not changed his mind?

In their hearts humans plan their course, but the LORD establishes their steps (Proverbs 16:9).

Escape to London

1. Dr Johnson told someone that Hannah was a flatterer. This hurt her feelings but maybe it was a little bit true. Why do you think Hannah flattered people? Are you ever tempted to do the same?

2. Hannah placed her hopes on her fame and her career. Can you imagine how she felt when people didn't like her plays? What happens when we build our lives on other people's opinions of us?

Humble yourselves before the Lord, and he will lift you up (James 4:10).

A New Book

1. Throughout her life, Hannah often fell ill when she had too much work to do or if something sad happened. She came to value these times because they made her rely on God more. How do you feel when you are ill or very tired or sad? Maybe next time something difficult happens in your life you could make a list of things to thank God for.

2. Hannah read John Newton's words, 'The Lord ... returns to convince, humble, pardon, comfort, and renew the soul,' and began to realise that however good she was, she still needed God to forgive her and change her. Are you trusting God to forgive you or are you trying to impress him with all the good things you do?

3. Many people looked down on Christians who took the Bible seriously in Hannah's day, just as they do in our day. What would you say to a friend who was scared to believe in Jesus because of what others might say?

But even if you should suffer for what is right, you are blessed.
'Do not fear their threats; do not be frightened' (1 Peter 3:14).

Trying Hard

1. When she built her first country cottage, Cowslip Green, Hannah thought that being in a peaceful place would make her more able to please God. Do you think our surroundings help us serve God? Why, or why not?

2. Ann Yearsley was a woman who'd had a hard life and was hard to help. Why do you think Hannah wanted to help her? What would you have done to help? What do you think Hannah learned through her experience with Ann?

Love ... always protects, always trusts, always hopes, always perseveres (1 Corinthians 13:7).

Changing the World

1. Hannah loved spending time with her friends at Teston. They had so much in common, but they didn't keep all their privileges to themselves. Look through the chapter and see how many ways they helped other people.

2. Lady Margaret Middleton was a very quiet and calm woman, very different from Hannah, but she had a great influence on other people. Who are you most like? How do you think the Lord can use your personality to help other people?

3. When he rode through a new area, William Wilberforce noticed things that other people didn't see. Next time you walk through your neighbourhood try to look at it with different eyes; ask yourself:

- Are there people in need?
- What are the homes like?
- Do many people live on their own?
- What do the people in your neighbourhood most need?

And what does the LORD require of you? To act justly and to love mercy and to walk humbly with your God (Micah 6:8).

Back to School

1. Why is learning to read so important? Many missionaries around the world are involved in literacy (reading and writing projects) today. Why don't you find out about one and start to pray for the missionaries and their work.

2. Imagine you were a village child in one of the new Sunday Schools. Would you have wanted to learn to read?

3. Do you think Hannah and Patty's advice about teaching was wise? Does kindness really bring more results than harshness?

The law of the LORD is perfect, refreshing the soul. The statutes of the LORD are trustworthy, making wise the simple.

The precepts of the LORD are right, giving joy to the heart (Psalm 19:7-8).

Runaways and Revolutions

1. Why do you think Clementina wanted to run away from her school? What would you have said to her if you'd found out about her plans?

2. What do adverts tell us that girls should be interested in? Do you think those adverts are right? What do you think you should value most of all?

3. Do you want to be popular? What is good and bad about popularity?

Your beauty should not come from outward adornment, such as elaborate hairstyles and the wearing of gold jewellery or fine clothes. Rather, it should be that of your inner self, the unfading beauty of a gentle and quiet spirit, which is of great worth in God's sight (1 Peter 3:3-4).

More Stories

1. Do you enjoy reading stories or watching TV? Perhaps your parents sometimes tell you there are some books or programmes you can't look at. Why do you think they say that? Are there any books or programmes which help you obey God more?

2. Have you ever been teased or criticised for following Jesus? Hannah learned to care less about her reputation when she was attacked. What did you learn about God when it happened to you?

But one thing I do: forgetting what is behind and straining towards what is ahead, I press on towards the goal to win the prize for which God has called me heavenwards in Christ Jesus (Philippians 3:13b-14)

The Final Chapter

1. In the last ten years of her life, Hannah had to stay at home. That didn't mean she was lonely though! She had lots of visitors and wrote and received thousands of letters. It is even easier for us today – we can email and text people too! Are there any people you know who find it hard to get out? Maybe they are ill or elderly. Can you visit or write to them? Perhaps, like some of the young people Hannah kept in touch with, you will be blessed by what they can tell you!

2. Hannah worked hard to improve the lives of others, but more than anything else she worked to enable men, women, boys and girls to meet the Lord Jesus in his Word, the Bible. Can you think of any new ways you can share God's love with others today?

Therefore, as God's chosen people, holy and dearly loved, clothe yourselves with compassion, kindness, humility, gentleness and patience (Colossians 3:12).

About the Author

Since coming to faith in Christ in her early teens, Sarah Allen has been to University, taught English, got married, had children and with her husband and family is now involved in a church plant in Huddersfield in the United Kingdom. The messiness of life with five children and a busy diverse church repeatedly leads Sarah back to the cross. "My walk with the Lord doesn't feel like a triumphant progress; but the Lord is so good to me, not one of His promises has ever failed."

Did You Know?

- When Hannah More was born, rich ladies wore hoop petticoats with strips of wood sewn in. These went under their skirts and held out their grand dresses. The largest were one and half metres wide! You would have had to go through doors sideways! By the time Hannah died, petticoats had gone out of fashion ... and come back in again, this time with metal strips sewn in.

- Girls and women had very few rights in eighteenth-century England. Single women could own money or houses but as soon as they got married all their belongings became their husband's. Only men who owned property could vote. Poor women did paid work but no one would have expected the wife of a wealthy man to earn money.

- The state education system in the United Kingdom stems from the schools like Hannah More's which were set up by individual Christians or churches. When the government said that all children had to go to school in 1870 it took over or funded many of the Christian schools which already existed.

- 'Methodist' was the name given to men and women who became Christians through the preaching of John and Charles Wesley beginning in the 1740s, around the time of Hannah's birth. This was a time of great revival when many, like Hannah More, had their lives turned around when they heard of the free forgiveness that comes through the cross. Some stayed within the Church of England, but others formed their own denomination known as 'Methodism'.

- Some historians think that it was the revival of Christianity in the eighteenth-century which prevented a bloody revolution (like the one in France) in England. Many workers became Christians and protested peacefully for change in very difficult times instead of rising against the government.

- Scottish Law allowed girls as young as twelve to be married without their parents' permission and with only two witnesses. In Gretna Green, the blacksmith often conducted weddings in his shop!

- In the Mendips, where most of Hannah's schools were, children worked hard, just like their parents. Some of them had to go down mines, and some of the mines started in the street or in houses. Imagine sitting down to tea next to a dark hole in the ground!

- If you live in the United Kingdom or in North America, some of the wealth you enjoy comes from slavery. Slave dealers and owners became extremely rich in the eighteenth century and their money was used to help the new factories which sprang up and to improve farming techniques. These countries grew richer and richer and we still enjoy the benefits today. Some countries lived in by the descendants of slaves say that the United Kingdom and other slaving nations should pay them compensation. What do you think?

- Hannah loved the theatre, but it was a dangerous place, for the actors at least! If the audience didn't like what they saw they might throw apples or oranges onto the stage!

- Slavery, in the form that Hannah knew, ended in the British Territories in 1833. There are other forms of slavery which still exist today around the world and closer to home; children are sold as workers to pay off their parents' debts; immigrants are trapped into working and their wages taken away by their handlers. Christians are campaigning against this, just as William Wilberforce and Hannah More were. Perhaps you can get involved too.

Hannah More Timeline

1739   George Whitefield and John Wesley start preaching in the open air.

1743   George II leads his army into battle; he is the last British king to do this.

1745   Hannah More born at Fishponds, outside Bristol.

1758   Mary More opens her boarding school in Bristol.

1760   Slaves revolt against their masters in Jamaica; they are defeated and 400 slaves die. George III crowned.

1762   Hannah visits William Taylor's home, Belmont and later in the year becomes engaged to him.

1771   Britains first cotton mill opens; the factory age has begun; Captain Cook 'discovers' Australia.

1773   Hannah's engagement is finally broken off.

1774   Hannah travels to London with Patty and meets David Garrick, the famous actor.

1775   Her first play is performed at a Theatre in Bath. American War of Independence begins.

1779   David Garrick dies, her third play is a disaster.

1780   Hannah reads *Cardiphonia*, a Christian book by John Newton and commits herself to Christ.

1782   *Sacred Dramas*, a book of plays based on Bible stories, is published.

1785   Hannah moves into her first house, Cowslip Green.

1786	Hannah gets involved with the movement against slavery.
1787	Hannah meets William Wilberforce and John Newton.
	First ships of convicts sail to Australia.
1788	Parliament investigates the slave trade.
1789	Hannah and Patty open their first school in the Mendips.
	French Revolution begins.
1791	Clementina Clerke elopes. Parliament rejects William Wilberforce's bill to abolish the slave trade.
1793	Britain goes to war with France.
1795	Hannah starts writing cheap story-leaflets.
1799	Hannah writes a book about girls' education.
1799	Three years of argument about the school in Blagdon begins.
1807	Britain abolishes the slave trade.
1811	Protesters called Luddites attack factory machines in protest against unemployment.
1815	Britain defeats France at the battle of Waterloo.
1819	Patty dies.
1820	George III dies and is followed by George IV.
1825	Hannah publishes her last book, *The Spirit of Prayer*.
1830	George IV dies and his brother becomes William IV.
1833	Abolition of slavery in all British territories.
	Factory Act brings fairer work hours for women and children.
	Hannah More dies.
1837	The Victorian age begins; King William dies and eighteen-year-old Victoria is crowned.

CHRISTIAN FOCUS PUBLICATIONS

Christian Focus | Christian Heritage | CF4K | Mentor

Christian Focus Publications publishes books for adults and children under its four main imprints: Christian Focus, CF4K, Mentor and Christian Heritage. Our books reflect our conviction that God's Word is reliable and Jesus is the way to know him, and live for ever with him.

Our children's publication list includes a Sunday School curriculum that covers pre-school to early teens, and puzzle and activity books. We also publish personal and family devotional titles, biographies and inspirational stories that children will love.

If you are looking for quality Bible teaching for children then we have an excellent range of Bible stories and age-specific theological books.

From pre-school board books to teenage apologetics, we have it covered!

Find us at our web page:
www.christianfocus.com

CF4•K
Because you're never too young to know Jesus